20
87f

St. Norbert College Library
DePere, WI

THE FREE SOCIETY

By

Clare E. Griffin

March 1965

PUBLISHED AND DISTRIBUTED BY THE

American Enterprise Institute
for Public Policy Research
Washington, D.C.

© 1965 American Enterprise Institute for Public Policy Research. 1200 17th Street, N.W., Washington, D. C. 20036 All rights reserved under International and Pan-American Copyright Conventions. Library of Congress Catalog No. 65-15709.

AMERICAN ENTERPRISE INSTITUTE
For Public Policy Research

THE AMERICAN ENTERPRISE INSTITUTE FOR PUBLIC POLICY RESEARCH, established in 1943, is a nonpartisan research and educational organization which studies national policy problems.

Institute publications take two major forms:

1. LEGISLATIVE AND SPECIAL ANALYSES—factual analyses of current legislative proposals and other public policy issues before the Congress prepared with the help of recognized experts in the academic world and in the fields of law and government. A typical analysis features: (1) pertinent background, (2) a digest of significant elements, and (3) a discussion, pro and con, of the issues. The reports reflect no policy position in favor of or against specific proposals.

2. LONG-RANGE STUDIES—basic studies of major national problems of significance for public policy. The Institute, with the counsel of its Advisory Board, utilizes the services of competent scholars, but the opinions expressed are those of the authors and represent no policy position on the part of the Institute.

ADVISORY BOARD

PAUL W. MCCRACKEN, *Chairman*
Professor, School of Business Administration, University of Michigan

KARL BRANDT
Professor of Economic Policy (emeritus)
Stanford University

MILTON FRIEDMAN
Paul S. Russell Distinguished Service Professor of Economics
University of Chicago

GOTTFRIED HABERLER
Galen L. Stone Professor of International Trade
Harvard University

FELIX MORLEY
Editor and Author

STANLEY PARRY
Professor, Department of Political Science
University of Notre Dame

E. BLYTHE STASON
Dean Emeritus, Law School
University of Michigan

GEORGE E. TAYLOR
Director, Far Eastern & Russian Institute
University of Washington

OFFICERS

Chairman
Carl N. Jacobs

Vice Chairmen
Walter C. Beckjord　Henry T. Bodman　H. C. Lumb

President
William J. Baroody

Treasurer
Henry T. Bodman

TRUSTEES

Henry W. Balgooyen
Walter C. Beckjord
Henry T. Bodman
Harry L. Bradley
John M. Briley
Robert P. Burroughs
Fuller E. Callaway, Jr.
Wallace E. Campbell
L. M. Cassidy
J. D. Stetson Coleman
Clyde T. Foster
Harry C. Hagerty
Walter Harnischfeger
John B. Hollister
Robert A. Hornby
N. Baxter Jackson
Carl N. Jacobs
Edward H. Little
Raymond S. Livingstone
Fred F. Loock
H. C. Lumb
William L. McGrath
George P. MacNichol, Jr.
Allen D. Marshall
H. S. Middendorf
Don G. Mitchell
Peter O'Donnell, Jr.
Harvey Peters
H. Ladd Plumley
Edmund W. Pugh, Jr.
Philip A. Ray
Herman J. Schmidt
William T. Taylor
R. C. Tyson
Errett Van Nice

Thomas F. Johnson
Director of Research

Joseph G. Butts
Director of Legislative Analysis

Earl H. Voss
Director of International Studies

Howard Friend
Director of Public Finance Analysis

FOREWORD

This study is not a discussion of any one of the economic problems of the day, such as the farm problem, unemployment, or the preservation of competition. And still we hope it will have a bearing on all of these. For here we propose to talk about principles and a certain philosophy of society and its government. Inevitably current problems will be mentioned, but only as a means of illustrating and giving substance to an otherwise disembodied philosophy, not with the intention of recommending detailed solutions.

This essay is not partisan in the sense of advocating a political party. It is intended to present a long-standing philosophy variously suggested, though not adequately defined, as free enterprise, free society or "liberalism" in the old classic sense. There are supporters of this philosophy in both major political parties of this country and certainly there are in both parties many who would reject these principles in fact even if not in word. This is not to say that the philosophy we hope to expound lacks limits, that it is so fuzzy that it can be accepted by all. Anyone who holds to this liberal philosophy can recognize his ideological friends and enemies. This is merely to say that not all his friends nor all his enemies will be found in one party.

Such a philosophy will have many facets and in its application it will, of course, touch many practical political questions. It is conceivable in some societies that not only a general philosophy but its applications could be expressed and unanimously accepted as party doctrine. But in a system of free speech and free political alignment it is only natural that very few people would accept all the features that logically attach to any "position statement," even when it deals only with broad concepts of government. Much less is it likely that many people can be enlisted in the support of any one detailed list of positions on current questions.

Hence, if a commentator attempts to delineate a philosophy of society in its several aspects and applications he may have difficulty in finding even one person besides himself who would endorse every feature. Can any one then set forth a general philosophy that expresses anything more than his personal preference? It should not be impossible, for there are certain ideas that are logically consistent. We shall try to start with some central concepts and then try to show that certain corollaries and applications naturally flow from them. We will find that, in general, though with notable exceptions, people's attitudes on social questions do form a logical pattern. What we seek here is the pattern of ideas that seem to be consistent with a free society or, more narrowly, a free enterprise system.

CONTENTS

I.

WHY DO WE NEED A PHILOSOPHY?

Americans are pre-eminently a practical people—not in the sense that our decisions are in fact always the most effective; but rather that, when we are faced by a problem, it is our inclination to tackle it vigorously with whatever solution seems promising, without much regard to an underlying philosophy or theory. This emphasis on the particular problem and a search for the most speedy solution of it has served us well in many ways. In the field of technology, for example, our great progress in the past has been based on "Yankee ingenuity." It did not in general depend heavily on genuine science, but on cut and try methods, or, as the expression goes, "thinking by the seat of your pants."

Eli Whitney did not employ any newly discovered principles of physics nor knowledge of the nature of matter to invent the cotton gin, which revolutionized the textile industry of the world. Nor did Edison rely on science. His efforts to find a filament for an incandescent lamp consisted of unsystematic persistence in "try this and try that." This approach "worked," and indeed it still does work in many areas all of the time and in all areas some of the time.

But in recent years there is a growing tendency for invention to be based on general science. Thus the atomic bomb could hardly have been invented by an unguided cut and try process. Rather, the advance in knowledge of the nature of matter culminating in the basic equation of $E = MC^2$ (expressing a basic relation of mass and energy) preceded and, it would seem, had to precede practical application. Incidentally, this reversed the old order of the expansion of knowledge not only here but generally for mankind. We used to find first how to do a thing and then perhaps much later find why it worked as, for example, men learned how to sail ships long before they learned about the principles of aerodynamics.

All this suggests an analogy with our task of dealing with the many problems that arise in a society. Where new problems are popping up continually we should have some basic ideas to apply to all of them or at least to broad areas. Perhaps we could use the current and overworked term, "guidelines." Actually we are inclined to seek solutions to our problems without much regard for consistency. For example, the same government agency may work for the preservation of competition in some cases and for limitation of competition in others, depending on what the particular administrators feel will work best or the relative strength of interested political groups.

Maybe our "catch-as-catch-can" approach is all right—that general principles ought to grow out of particular decisions, if indeed they are to be recognized at all. But it seems that with our very complex society and with the larger number of questions that statecraft is called upon to answer, we should refer back to some broad and well grounded general propositions. We are in a position not dissimilar from that of modern science and technology in that we cannot safely continue to rely on pure improvisation in social and political affairs any more than the technologist in some of our newer fields can proceed without knowledge of the basic science.

Statesmen of our early years as a nation were more concerned with broad principles. For example, the authors of the *Federalist Papers* dealt with the principles of federalism and they were concerned with such broad questions as how order and freedom could be combined in society. But today the question of the proper role of the central and local government and its significance for a free society does not apparently occupy much time and attention from those who are eager to settle some troublesome current problem. The tendency seems to be for the reformers to work through that unit of government that gives most promise of settling the particular problem in a way satisfactory to them.

In practice this often means use of the national government. There are several reasons for this bias. For one thing, if you can get your reform measure adopted by the national government, you save a lot of time compared to the tedious process of getting action of 50 states. So it happens that the conservatives who oppose the proposal are put in the role of supporting the states rights and the reformers seem to be on the side of strong central government. It is possible that the preservation or even careful re-defining of the proper roles of local and central government is, in the long run, more important than the proposed solution of current problems. But it is not surprising, for example, that persons who are completely absorbed in getting their solution to racial problems adopted and enforced would regard the states rights arguments as either inspired by blind prejudice or hopelessly academic and "old fashioned." And one must confess that many of the "states righters" are no more profound students of political theory than the advocates of powerful central government. Nor, as another example, have I observed that such a basic consideration as the future of our federal system has any noticeable effect on a university administrator who is hot on the trail of a new and larger grant from Washington.

We have here deliberately used examples of very worthwhile ends. Indeed equality of opportunity, which is involved in the race question and also in the expansion of educational opportunities, is a fundamental value. But so also is the division of powers represented by the state and Federal Government. Indeed many observers, present and past, believe that the principle of representative government can only be preserved in a large country like ours by the principles of federalism. We ought not to sacrifice the value of federalism for the value of equal opportunity until we are sure that this "agonizing choice" is inevitable, which in this case it surely is not.

We have noted that the Founding Fathers of this country did pay attention to general principles and a philosophy of government. We may add that in our present world the Communists also take the general philosophy and theory of government very seriously. Sometimes they carry it to the ridiculous extreme of condemning the advocates of new ideas as revisionists. And the heat generated by the clash between varieties of the revealed truth suggests an undesirable inflexibility. But the attention that is paid to basic doctrine and the respect for it is probably in the long run a source of strength.

Another reason for giving more thought to a social philosophy is that the problems of the day that need our attention are apparent and demanding, while the indirect effects of many of the remedies may be to impair some even more valuable ends. These greater values, individual freedom for example, can easily and quite unintentionally be eroded. Eternal vigilance, which we have been told is the price of liberty, does not refer merely or in these days mainly to guarding against some tyrant, domestic or foreign, who is plotting to take away our freedom. In its better sense it refers to the things we ourselves do in the effort to take care of lesser problems. An example is government price or wage fixing to avoid a strike. Preserving the continuity of production is, of course, good and its value is readily apparent. But the impairment of the free market system is bad. And it does strike at our freedoms much more than does an interruption of steel production, though its impact is not so apparent. It would seem that in the midst of controversy on practical issues it might be well to pause to consider what are some of the features of a free society and some of the requirements for its preservation.

II.

MAN AND SOCIETY

Much has been written by sociologists and others on the nature of society. The Germans have been especially prone to ascribe an existence and a character to a society which transcends that of the people who are included in it. In some cases these views lead to a concept of a society or a state as an organism which is different and greater than the sum of the people included, just as the human body is something more than the sum of the cells which constitute it. Obviously such an analogy glorifies the state. Correspondingly it minimizes the individual.

The sum of all the cells may make up an admirable body. But no one cell which, together with several others, constitutes only the tip of a little finger, can be accounted of great importance. Moreover, the cell in an organism has no reason for existence except as it serves the whole body. The theories of Heinrich von Treitschke and other German writers along these lines, in the latter half of the nineteenth century, helped lay an ideological basis for national socialism.

This is an intriguing line of thought, but we will bypass it here and accept a non-mystical concept of society. In this view, the essence of a society is interdependence. More than that, it must be interdependence which is recognized. So a group of people whose actions or nonactions affect each other, and who in their actions take account of this fact, is a society.

Before the modern geographic discoveries, several parts of the world had no contact, peaceful or warlike. One can hardly apply the term "family of man" to this situation. An instance in ancient times was the dependence of Rome upon China for silk, in spite of the fact that the existence of China was not known to the Romans and probably Rome was not known to China. The silk was carried westward a few hundred miles by one trader and there passed on to another trader. And so, like a series of links in a chain, the silk finally came to the eastern Mediterranean, where it entered into the commerce of the Roman world. In the view of a Roman, therefore, silk came from Asia Minor. Under these conditions, it would be inaccurate to speak of a society which encompassed Rome and China, in spite of an actual but unrecognized interdependence. But today nearly all people do rely upon other countries. They are aware of it and, to some extent at least, adjust their actions to this fact. To the extent that they do, we have a world society.

But here we are more directly concerned with a national society or perhaps one covering related countries, as e.g., Western society. What is the reason for this focus? In society, in this sense, questions arise as to the proper scope, authority, and activity of the society and the individual. In modern times, society is chiefly represented by the state, which is society politically organized, and even more specifically, by the organized government, which is the mechanism set up by the state.[1]

---

[1] There are various views of the relation of society, state, and government. One view is that society and state are opposed organizations of people, the former relying upon voluntary action, the latter upon force. Mr. Felix Morley, if I understand him correctly, holds to this concept and expresses it in his *Freedom and Federalism,* p. 30 and passim (Chicago: Henry Regnery Co. 1959). My own view is that society is the broader concept, including all the people related as described above. This society develops and imposes morals, taboos, and in general defines a civilization. Its members organize themselves or get organized in many ways, such as in a system of domestic relations, a market system, a religious system—the church or churches and into the state for the use of coercion either to enforce morals which are generally held by the society or objectives which the state itself originates. The state then is society organized in one of its many ways. I would think of the relation of society and state in this way rather than as two parallel and rival entities. It is true that any one of the organizations of society may

The distinction of state and government is worth noting, for many thinkers would agree that the sovereignty of the state is unlimited while in a free society, the powers of government should be strictly defined and limited. To say that the sovereign power of the state is unlimited is merely to assert the rather obvious fact that the people as a whole can exert maximum power, limited only by an appeal to natural rights or divinely established rights of man. In the United States this ultimate sovereign power lies in the people, organized in constitutional conventions or other means of establishing or amending the organic law. It is this organic law, largely embodied in our Constitution, that creates the government and defines its powers.

A recognition of this all-powerful state, on the one side, and of limits placed on the powers of government and of rights assured to people no matter how small a minority they may be, on the other, has led some to view with admiration and amazement this form of society, which is now so new in the history of the world and so rare. José Ortega y Gasset, Spanish political philosopher, has expressed this admiration more eloquently than have those who, living under such a system, have lost the sense of wonderment: He writes:

> The political doctrine which has represented the loftiest endeavor towards common life is liberal democracy. It carries to the extreme the determination to have consideration for one's neighbor. . . . Liberalism is that principle of political rights, according to which the public authority, in spite of being all-powerful, limits itself and attempts, even at its own expense, to leave room in the state over which it rules for those to live who neither think nor feel as it does, that is to say, as do the stronger, the majority. Liberalism—it is well to recall this today—is the supreme form of generosity; it is the right which the majority concedes to minorities and hence it is the noblest cry that has ever resounded in this planet. It announces the determination to share existence with the enemy; more than that, with an enemy which is weak. It was incredible that the human species would have arrived at so noble an attitude, so paradoxical, so refined . . . so anti-natural.[2]

---

extend its power to submerge the others as, for example, in some societies the church dominates all phases of life and in some others the market-place with its rules and objectives has approached that position.

I surely share with Mr. Morley a hearty dislike of coercion and a concern about its modern day extension by the state or, more narrowly, by the government. We must recognize, however, the possibilities of coercion or near-coercion possessed by society in its other forms, such as the church, public opinion, and custom, as was so well shown by J. S. Mill in his *Essay on Liberty*.

[2] José Ortega y Gasset, *The Revolt of the Masses* (translation; New York: W. W. Norton & Co., 1932), p. 83.

But why are these limitations which the majority places upon itself so admirable? Generous—yes, but is it not a weak spined concession? If the state or directors thereof are right, why do they allow error in views or actions of an antisocial kind to stand in the way of attaining the City of God. Hitler and his National Socialists, Mussolini and his Fascists, and Stalin and his Communists saw only weakness and "decadence of the West" in this generosity.

For the most part we do believe in these limits on government. Why? The answer has to go, I believe, to the nature of the human beings who are the entities that make up the society. One of the features of a human being is that he is an individual in the true sense that he is unique. There is no other one exactly like him. It seems, perhaps, because of our vantage point as a human being, that this uniqueness is more pronounced among humans than in any other species of living creatures. We cannot prove it, but so it seems. Also he has, more than others, the capacity for making choices (decisions), where lesser breeds in the family of living creatures are to a greater degree ruled by instincts and inherited characteristics. This ability to choose is the essence of humanity. It exists at a low level with children and it deveolps as the person grows. The ability to choose between this course and that gives a basis for the concepts of right and wrong. Moral judgments on nonliving things are not possible, and they are decidedly limited in the case of slaves or of children still under their parents' authority. Man becomes good or evil only when he has the power to choose. Knowing good and evil and having the power of choice, he is no longer a thing; he has become a free agent—that is to say in its richest meaning, a man.

It is, therefore, a requirement of his nature to grow—to grow in sensitivity, in perception and discrimination, in intellect and in willingness, and in capacity for accepting responsibilities. These are the attributes of a mature person. It is these that justify the assertion "Thou hast made him but little lower than the angels." The ideal is that the process of change from childhood to maturity should be continuous. It should be the "permanent revolution."

We who live with and accept the values of Western civilization assert that organized society is an instrumentality of men and that it shall be organized in such a way as to serve the needs of men. This is a pretty big proposition, and except in a few instances like the golden age of Greece it has only been seriously asserted since the seventeenth century. The opposite view has been more common, for example, that man exists for the state or for other objectives to which even the state is subordinate. This might be the glory of God or of several gods, the glory and prestige of a ruling individual or family or class. But though logic fails at this point, we do accept the pre-eminence of individuals. They are the end; the state is the means.

If this article of faith be accepted, the next question naturally presents itself, namely, what form of society will be most conducive to the advancement of the individuals in it? Well, if our previous paragraphs are even approximately correct the answer must be: that form of society which in the maximum degree will permit and even encourage individuals to make their own decisions and which only in the minimum will direct their activities and relieve them of decisions.

The range of choice which men have is, of course, partly determined by the organization of their society. But it is also determined by the natural environment, by man's knowledge and his technology, his supply of capital (the result of past savings), and by other circumstances. The significant feature of the physical environment in the modern world is that it reduces the barriers to free choice, which in the past inhibited his freedom of choice. When an environment is excessively hard and overbearing, the freedom of man to think, to experiment, in short, to become a full-blown individual, is limited by nature itself. The Eskimo who faces the problem of making a living on the ice is in that position. He thus has what Arnold Toynbee calls an arrested civilization. On the other hand nature may be so lush and kind that it presents an inadequate challenge, and this too encourages a static or declining civilization. In neither of these is it a faulty social organization which is solely or probably chiefly responsible for slow cultural development.

But we, i.e., modern people of Western civilization, have in these external factors a most favorable situation. Science and technology have greatly extended our mastery of nature, we are past the fear of starvation and dire want. This shifts the question of human freedom, freedom of choice and hence the condition of human growth, onto our own capacity to appreciate the needs of a good society and to set up the government of it. If we miss this opportunity it will be our own fault. In this great question we collectively have the power of decision.

We have said that the making of decisions will develop man to his greatest potential. Now we see the cumulative effect of this process, for a high degree of human maturity and development is conducive to the making of wise decisions in this very large problem of setting up the good society.

Before we gained this degree of mastery over nature, the need for goods was so urgent that for practical purposes and in most parts of the world one could measure economic and social progress merely by the supply of certain standard goods available to the individuals in that society. But as we have advanced our productivity to a point where minimum physical needs are met, the concept of well-being can be broadened to include the satisfactions that inhere in freedom of action for its own sake. We can now choose our social forms not merely by their effectivness in making a living, but also in making us free in the broadest sense.

III.

WHAT IS THE GOOD SOCIETY?

If we adhere to that concept of a good society which is basic to Western civilization, that it is one that best advances the interests of its members; and if we remember that the members of that society want very different things and in different proportions; it follows that the good society will have only certain minimum and general objectives of its own. Its chief objective will be to create an environment in which the individuals will be able to select and to pursue *their own objectives*. This seems inescapable. But then we come back to the fact that the possibility of attaining the material goods, more refined and varied services, and leisure—this depends upon the actions of others and upon the effective integration of those activities. Taking these facts and aspirations into account, we can then state our objective as follows: *to facilitate and to encourage the development of the inherent abilities and potentialities of individuals and to improve the interrelations of people so that they may, to an ever growing degree, realize the ends that to them individually seem important.* To the extent that we make progress on this road, men will become free, not merely in the minimum and important sense of being free from the arbitrary rule of man over man, but in the positive sense of realizing their own potentialities and attaining the life that they seek for themselves.

It is perhaps not necessary to add that this is not a vision of anarchy. Clearly, the maximizing of the freedom of all individuals to seek their own ends requires that all of them shall be limited in such actions as would reduce the freedoms of others. The ideal is a net increase in freedom. This concept of a *net* increase of freedom is needed to bring together those whose sole ideal is freedom and those, on the other hand, who urge the need for controls. The fact is that we cannot judge a particular restraint in its effect on freedom until we look at the indirect or surrounding facts. For example, for the police to install a stoplight at a street intersection appears to restrict my freedom to pass that corner any time as I please. But in its larger effect, a well-planned system of stoplights can add to my freedom to get from one part of the city to another expeditiously.

In making this point the defender of freedom should take care that he does not concede too much. The concession made here would not justify the reduction in freedom merely for the sake of increased efficiency. We must insist that people must have the right to make their own mistakes. The traffic illustration implies that freedom itself has been preserved—perhaps increased. The state here is not deciding for me where I should go, or, indeed, whether I should go any place. It enables me to make my own choice and makes it easier for me to carry it out. This *prima facie* limitation on my freedom has increased my net freedom.

Life is full of such paradoxes. Schumpeter,[1] for example, remarks that brakes are obviously designed to slow the speed of a car, yet the development of better brakes has no doubt contributed to the higher speeds at which we drive, as truly as have the more powerful engines. Likewise progress may be made by checks upon it. A patent is designed to prevent producers generally from freely adopting a known improvement, which would represent progress. This protection of the inventor or owner of the patent is designed and probably does foster

---

[1] Joseph Schumpeter, *Capitalism, Socialism and Democracy* (New York: Harper & Brother, 1942).

progress. It is considerations such as these that distinguish a modern sophisticated philosophy of freedom from crude laissez faire and the old aphorism, "that that government is best which governs least." The difference between government action that is favorable to a free society or opposed to it is not mainly in the *amount* of legislation or even of administration but in its direction and purpose. For example, economic freedom may be enhanced by regulations and policies aimed at prevention of fraud. The essential question to ask in each case is: "Will this measure in its total effect increase or diminish the freedom of individuals, taking into account both degree of effect and number of individuals?"

Another caution is that an increase in freedom does not imply that the individuals will be insensitive to the rights and needs of others—quite the contrary. Generosity in such a society does not cease to be a virtue. Indeed, as Ortega has reminded us, the conception that the sovereign power, the majority, shall preserve to the weak and defenseless the right to their own values and the right to seek them in their own way is the highest form of generosity. But these provisos are not intended to weaken the objective as stated. *A good society will be one in which as many people as possible will be as free as possible to seek as successfully as possible the ends that to them seem good.*

IV.

A FREE SOCIETY AND FREE ENTERPRISE

So much for the ideal of a free society. The relation of free enterprise to it is twofold: first, that the general freedom to seek one's ends in such ways as one chooses—as long as they do not infringe upon the freedom of others—includes a number of such mundane things as the freedom to choose between operating as an independent entrepreneur, i.e., running your own business, or working for another; and, second, that free enterprises—conducted, as they must be, with due regard to the wishes of consumers, workers, and investors, as expressed in the market—will advance the freedom of choice of all these others. That these freedoms can never be perfectly attained is clear. The ideal of a free society and of free enterprise as a part of it is to be envisaged as a road, not as a destination that has been reached. On this road there is plenty of room for progress, for reform, for growth, and for adventure.

Let us revert for a moment to the proposition that a free society will have few objectives of its own, and note that it has been disregarded by many statesmen of both major parties in recent years. A few years ago there was much talk to the effect that as a nation we had lost our sense of direction and that we needed to define our national goals. Without arguing the merit of these views at this point, we can observe that this is quite different from the view that it is individual people or voluntary groups of them who should have specific goals. It is the proper role of government to maintain an environment in which they can pursue these goals. This, of course, is itself a very important goal for government. The goal is to advance human freedom including, very importantly, economic freedom. But the people who were bemoaning our lack of national purpose would surely not be satisfied with that. From the point of view of political leaders it sounds like a negative policy because it might well call for less government action rather than more. Their desire for a national purpose would not be satisfied by creating a favorable environment and then sitting by to see what a free people brought forth. What the American people have brought forth in the past two centuries is pretty startling in the history of the world. But no one decided what their collective goal was to be, and it would be quite impossible, even after the events, to give a clear-cut statement of the national goals that have dominated our society.

Among the proposed goals, the currently fashionable one is economic growth as measured by an increase in gross national product at some specified rate per year. The growth of an economy can generally be presumed to be good when it comes as the natural result of voluntary effort and action of the people. This is quite a different matter from the government adopting a policy and specific steps to insure it. To do this may very well limit the freedom of the market, and the freedom of individuals, for example, to work more or less, to save or spend, and to exercise these freedoms foolishly or wisely as they themselves are foolish or wise. Whatever may be true of the growth of the GNP of a nation, it surely is true that if *individuals* are to grow they must preserve their rights to make their own mistakes. As long as these rights are preserved we cannot assure economic growth according to a blueprint.

The way of growth of a free system may, therefore, appear haphazard, though we may remark in passing that it is more likely to present that appearance to the uninitiated than to the serious student of economic science. But the natural rate of growth may be higher than the organized rate, whether we look at the short run or the long run. The recovery of West Germany after its controls had been swept away by the new economic minister, Ludwig Erhard, and after the mark had been stabilized by the Americans under General Clay is a case in point. The rate of growth was so much greater after these events than before and so much greater in Germany than in the other countries of Western Europe which were deeply immersed in their quotas, price controls, and other paraphernalia that the pragmatic case for a free market was greatly enhanced. Socialism of the democratic economic planning type (as opposed to thoroughgoing communism) received a setback in prestige from which it has not recovered. Some observers have said with much basis of truth that the socialism of Western Europe is intellectually bankrupt. But it is hard for those who never did understand the intricate automaticity of a free market to accept this free-wheeling growth. It seems that to satisfy them the growth must be planned. They admire the neatness and tidiness of a well groomed park more than the exuberant disorganization of nature. In terms of economic philosophy they admire order more than freedom. They would not appreciate the dictum of Henry David Thoreau, "In wildness is the preservation of the world."

V.

INTERDEPENDENCE AND FREEDOM

So far in our discussion of the philosophy of a free society we have stressed the pre-eminence of the individual and his freedom, and the essentially subordinate place of the group. This concept standing by itself, however, is but one of two essential points. The other idea is the interdependence of people in a modern society—particularly their economic interdependence. It is the conflict or interaction of these two that creates the central problem of a free society.

The United States and, indeed, all the countries of Western civilization are facing this problem which in degree, and to some extent in kind, is unprecedented in the history of the world. Upon the satisfactory solution of it depends the future of free societies. This central problem is that of reconciling the fact of economic interdependence with the aspiration for individual freedom.

The people of these countries and of the United States in particular are more highly interdependent than ever before. This mutual dependence has greatly increased in the last 150 years as a result of the progress of the industrial revolution, the growth of markets, and the domination of men's affairs by the requirements of the market and of modern methods of production and distribution. This growing dependence of one upon all has expanded in a number of directions. It has expanded geographically, as is shown by the fact that the economic activities and fortunes of the people of one part of our country are importantly affected by the activities of others, and, likewise, that the economic facts and policies of other countries affect the individuals of this country. The logic of the machine and of the market has thus brought into actuality at least one aspect of the vision of philosophers and religious teachers—the realization that no man can live to himself alone.

This mutual dependence is also shown in the relations of occupational and functional groups. The worker depends upon workers in other crafts and occupations, upon the suppliers of capital, upon the owners of resources, and upon business enterprisers; and all these depend for their success in turn upon the workers and upon each other. In this country, for example, some four out of five members of the labor force are employees, i.e., they work for others. Here the dependence on others is evident. Nor does the other fifth escape this interdependence, for insofar as they are themselves employers, they depend upon employees and suppliers; and even if they are self-employed in farming or in personal services, they are dependent upon the market. By comparison with the conditions of 100 years ago in this country, a larger proportion of our people are dependent upon the market; and in degree, they are more heavily dependent upon it.

There is no need to dwell here upon the beneficent results of this interrelated economy. It is clear enough that many more people are alive today than could have been under any previous system of production; and it is clear that, on the whole, they are living much better. The fear of starvation, which in earlier centuries oppressed large numbers in even the advanced nations, has been virtually abolished in those countries. A very large proportion of these people enjoy comforts which were previously available only to small privileged groups. And the fundamental security of person and assurance of subsistence has been greatly extended. All of these are gains to be credited to the modern economy. But this complex economy has also imposed new hazards in the increased degree to which the success or failure of the efforts of individuals depends upon the actions or inactions of others. Each has gained in significance for all.

But men live not merely by those material goods that are implied by "making a living." They can realize their ambitions only by freedom. This means not merely the rights of free thought, speech, and religion, but economic freedom, that is, the freedom to engage in this activity or that, to work more or less, to work here or there, and to spend the fruits of one's work as one sees fit. Some degree of such freedom of choice is essential to well-being. To have to accept goods that one wants less than other goods reduces satisfaction just as surely as would a general scarcity of all goods. As the minimum requirements of subsistence are met, this desire for free choice and self-determination increases; and, because of the gains already made, the ideal of free choice has become a practical goal for many people in the Western countries. The unique problem that faces our society is to reconcile interdependence and individual freedom. Any philosophy of a free society must provide for a solution of this problem.

It is evident that there can be no perfect solution. If a person were building a house under pioneer conditions, he would be independent and free; but his house would be a poor thing, and it would require very onerous and extended efforts. Today he will get an incomparably better house for less effort; but he will inevitably be less free in doing so because he is dependent upon others for materials, upon the demands of a dozen crafts, and upon local building restrictions. If he is to have the advantages of division of labor, he must, to some extent, accept the restrictions upon his freedom which such division implies.

So in various ways there are such clear advantages in division of labor that for economic reasons the vast majority of men will follow it if the opportunity is offered. But division of labor requires trade. Trade means contacts between otherwise isolated people. These contacts advance civilization.

And so there are important noneconomic effects of this division of labor. Over larger and larger areas we are coming to have a more or less homogeneous civilization. Commerce naturally produces this effect. As commerce develops cities lose their insularity. Ideas and fashions come in from outside with the trader and his wares. The stimulus of varied ideas produces advances in learning and the arts. And so, for example, in the cities of the ancient Greek world commerce and culture developed together. In that world those cities (Corinth, Athens, and Carthage) that participated in the great division of labor which was developing in the Mediterranean world advanced in art and civilized occupations, while those that were based on war—Sparta and Rome—became strong in an iron-fist way but they could only envy, though they pretended to scorn, the refinements of the commercial cities.

It is interesting to note that Karl Marx was well aware of these fruits of capitalism. Several passages in *The Communist Manifesto* are nothing short of glowing as to the achievements of capitalism in this respect. Even when pronouncing death sentence on capitalism he never failed to recognize its necessity in its time and the contribution it had made. He writes: "The bourgeosie (capitalism) draws all nations into civilization. It has created enormous cities and thus rescued a considerable part of the population from the idiocy (sic) of rural life. It has through its exploitation of the world market given a cosmopolitan character to production and consumption in every country. In place of the local and national seclusion and self-sufficiency we have intercourse in every direction, a universal interdependence of nations." [1]

Both Adam Smith, the prophet of free enterprise, in 1776, and Marx, the prophet of communism, in 1847, agreed that capitalism through extension of the principle of division of labor has created a real and ever more pervasive interdependence. And, moreover, they both admired this accomplishment, though they could differ on the future of the system which produced it. It is remarkable how many different people of such widely different social philosophies and from so many different starting points have come to the conclusion that "man cannot live to himself alone." These great thinkers give little support to a policy of isolationism. The traditional liberal philosophy has always favored freedom of trade, and absence of barriers to travel, and the exchange of ideas. It has always stood for the "open society." And so does the philosophy of a free market and a free society today.

So we see that the modern world owes much to the Siamese twins, division of labor and exchange. Adam Smith rested his case for free trade partly on the fact that the extent of division of labor depended upon the extent of the market. This combination, as we have seen, has been very fruitful in material and non-material ways such as interchange of ideas, advancement of arts and sciences, and, in the long run, we hope, an increase of tolerance and an economic argument for the futility of war and the logic of peace.

But as we come to rely upon others and they to rely upon us, freedom in its most obvious sense is affected. This is seen in many ways. The extreme of freedom in production would be when everyone could do exactly what he pleased. But it is quite evident that in an interdependent society there are limits to the realization of this desire. For somehow

[1] *The Communist Manifesto,* passim.

the productive efforts of the people as producers must be equated with the things desired by the people as consumers. What we as producers produce must be the same things and quantities that we as consumers consume. Considering the millions of producers on the one hand and the millions of consumers (same people) on the other it is indeed a notable acomplishment that a reasonably good match is effected.

Much progress was made particularly in the nineteenth century in developing this intricate system of exchange extending over the whole world. The most notable deviations from this broad line of progress have been made by the Socialists or planned-economy countries. The reason is quite clear. If any government aspires to control or to fix wages, prices, or other matters in the society, it must isolate itself from the effect of the world market. A country cannot be a part of the intricate world market system and enjoy the fruits of that system unless it is willing to accept the discipline of that market.

This is an example on a national scale of the fact that there is a basic conflict between interdependence and freedom. Nations as well as individuals must recognize the need for reconciling them.

Before discussing how we do reconcile the fact of interdependence with the desire for freedom, perhaps we should note the theoretical possibility of choosing one or the other and not attempting a reconciliation. Thus an individual could choose to reject the advantages of division of labor and to live the life of a hermit. He would remain "free" in the sense of avoiding man-made coercion. But he would have to content himself with low material standards of living. A nation can do the same thing with bad but not necessarily disastrous results depending on how large the country is and how much division of labor can exist within its borders.

How is this brought about? One could answer this simply by saying it is the functioning of the price system in the market place. This answer, which falls so easily from our lips, is true, but its very familiarity hides for us its importance. To jolt us into a recognition we might say that the answer to this question constitutes the most remarkable social development that the human race has yet brought about. For that answer is that men have developed an intricate system which accomplishes results that any man or group of administrators would find impossible. What are some of these requirements? This is really equivalent to asking what is *the* economic problem in general terms.

VI.

THE ECONOMIC FUNCTIONS

As remarked before, the economic problem can be viewed as that of achieving a reasonably good match between the output of people as producers with the demands of the people as consumers. Perhaps we should expand the question by asking what "reasonably good match" implies. The economic problem in its most general terms is how to reconcile two facts, namely, that human wants in the aggregate are insatiable and that the means of satisfying them are limited. Merely to state this general proposition implies that choices have to be made. If the means of satisfying wants were unlimited, there would be no problem because we would have as much as we wanted of everything. On the other hand, if the range of human wants were limited instead of being insatiable we would attain or look forward to attaining a time when all wants could be satisfied. All the pictures which have been painted of Utopia involve one or the other of these two situations. In the Garden of Eden, the wants were originally quite limited. There is a grave economic significance in the command that Adam and Eve should not eat of the tree of knowledge, which we perhaps can think of as the knowledge or imagination of things which we do not have. As soon as this knowledge came to them the fat was in the fire. The curse placed upon Adam that "thou shalt earn thy bread by the sweat of thy brow" was merely the recognition of an inevitable fact, as was also the banishment of the pair from the Garden by the angel with the flaming sword. When Eve had developed the desire for a fig leaf dress and no doubt a fig leaf hat (and who wants to wear the same hat all the time?), the economic future of the human race in broad terms had been pretty well determined.

But the existence of a perpetual problem is distasteful to some. The necessary efforts of mankind to solve the problem are rejected by these people as having no proper place in a good society. Wordsworth, for example, wrote: "Heaven abhors the lore/of the nicely calculated/ less or more." Good enough, but from what we can gather about heaven there (a) will be only limited wants or (b) unlimited means of satisfying wants. So his conclusion may well be correct. It may be that cost accountants and economists who are absorbed in the lore of costs and values, of the less and more, will find no professional employment there—if indeed they get there.

This sentiment of Wordsworth's suggests a reason for the low view which poets, religious leaders, and many others have of businessmen and the whole economic system—especially one which relies on economic incentives. But in spite of the wishful thinking or mere day dreams that would wave aside the economic problem, it is here. The question is: How do we make the best of the situation?

Well, what is required? We have here in a great nation, let us say, 100 million people whose labor can produce things. We also have 100 million people (the same people) who wish to consume things or obtain things for their dependents to consume. How do we get the two together? We obviously need methods of accomplishing several specific things. These are the several unavoidable functions that must be performed by any successful economic system.

In the first place we must recognize that people generally are inclined to be lazy, and in the second place that many of them desire security, that is, they would like to avoid risks. Somehow or other, then, we have to induce people who would rather sit in the shade to get up and work and, if we are to have progress, to induce people, at least some of them, to take risks. The first economic function, therefore, is to provide incentives (motivation). The incentive for work could be accomplished by a master-slave relationship, and the incentive for risk-taking by conferring the power of initiative upon some group in the community who were more adventurous or imaginative than the others. Or instead of the master with his lash we might try the more moderate device of providing rewards for work instead of punishment for not working, trying to induce people to work instead of loaf. In other words, we can use the carrot or the stick which, as has been said, are separately or in combination the only two known methods of making a donkey go forward. The incentive system applies both rewards and penalties, with more emphasis on the former as a society advances and becomes more affluent.

Second, we come to the question of what shall we produce. The answer in a good society is that we should produce the things that the people as consumers want. But that leaves the question of which people's desires are to be most heavily weighted. There are any number of ways in which these questions could be answered. I have heard it said in India, for example, that a Brahman has a right to be 11 times happier than other people. We might leave the decision of what is to be produced to the leaders. This is done in Russia and Red China. Or we might adopt the very simple plan that each person's vote would be of equal value. A refinement of this simple one man-one vote basis is our own in which the ballots are dollars and the voting power of each person is determined by his income. Under this system those goods will be produced for which there is a demand at a price which will be higher than the cost of producing the goods.

Third, there is the question of the distribution of income. The close relation between this and the previous question should be apparent for once you have decided who is to have the income you have presumably gone far in deciding what goods are to be produced. Some Socialists try to gloss over this problem and would permit differences in income but would reserve to the state the decision of what is to be produced. But it is of little value to individuals to have the income if they cannot spend it for the things which they desire. There are many bases on which distribution of income could be made. Our economic system, per se, tends to assign purchasing power to individuals in proportion to the values of his contribution to the requirements of the society as indicated by the market. From the point of view of social engineering, this is a neat solution, because it solves two problems at once, namely, the problem of incentives, and the problem of distribution. Notice that a non-market controlled society will face two separate problems, first, how to get work done and risks assumed, and, second, how to distribute the proceeds. We combine them.

Fourth, in connection with the question of what we shall produce there is the problem of allocation of resources. Our resources, natural and human, are limited. The question is, for example, shall we use our limited amount of iron ore for making this thing or that? The answer in our system is given by the price system. The makers of automobiles can meet their needs for steel if the product which they are selling will have sufficient value to the consumers to cover a price of steel which is as high or higher than that which would be yielded by any other use. In other words, industries and ultimately the people are again voting with their dollars.

Fifth, another question is: Who is going to be allowed to serve as the producer of different products? If we are to make the best use of our resources, it would seem that capable managers should be chosen and that the more capable managers would be put in charge of the larger amounts of resources or more valuable resources than would the less capable ones. In the field of agriculture, for example, the good farmers should get the good farm land.

It is true that some people would reason differently, namely, that the good farmer has a natural advantage over the others and, therefore, this should be compensated by giving him the poorer land and giving the richer land to the poorer farmers. This may appeal to some people on an equalitarian basis, but it is not likely to maximize desired output. If we do want to give the good land to the good farmers, the problem arises, how do you determine who are the good farmers? You could decide this by the amount of education that the farmer had had; you could give him a civil service examination; you might let him draw lots; you might give it to those farmers who first staked out their claims, as was done in the granting of new lands by the government; or you could decide it on the basis of the ability of the farmer to buy the land. This last one we employ, on the theory that good farmers will presumably earn more money on whatever land they have than will others. With this larger supply of money they will be in a better position to get control of the good land. This does not work precisely, of course, but generally observation seems to suggest that even if shiftless and poor farmers do get the rich land they do not long remain in control of it. These five functions have to be performed in any economy, regardless of its ideology, if it is going to be at all successful in bringing together the resources on the one side with the needs and desires on the other.

Sixth, if the society now wants to make progress there is still another necessary problem. That is how do you induce producers to change their ways if an industry is operating on a moderate but reasonably sure margin of profit. How do you get innovation?

In a controlled economy you might have a group of scientists and engineers who would devise better ways and, once these have been found they would be put into effect by decree. If the directors are very independent of the people, in other words if you have a well-established autocracy and if it happens that the autocrat is inclined to improvements and adventure, we might make progress by this means. In a controlled economy, however, which is responsible to any considerable degree to the people, the directors are likely to develop a high degree of conservatism on the theory that if the new plan does not work well they will be held responsible. If, on the other hand, they do not make this adventurous move, no one can criticize them, for they would be doing as well as could be expected in this industry; and the critics are not likely to know what the potentialities are. We do not need to speculate on this type of psychology. We have only to look at certain aspects of military organizations and of Civil Service activities.

Another way of getting progress is through a competitive system which promises high reward for either a new product or a higher profit from a new cost-reducing device. If the new product or service is feasible and has genuine value, it will, for the time being, yield an unusually good profit to the adventurer. If things do turn out this way, then the rest of the producing community will follow in his trail. If it does not turn out well, they shun the idea or drop it very quickly. So here is a system of progress using the price system in which strong incentive is given to make progress—strong enough to overcome the danger of loss, and to direct the whole industry into improved lines by the desire of the other producers to follow the successful experiments and to reject the failures.

A characterization of this system is expressed in an epigram by Professor Schumpeter, which many an economist wishes he had invented. In a system of capitalism, says he, "followers get leaders whom they do not want and leaders get followers whom they do not want." And thus, given the freedom of the uneasy ones and possibly of the dispossessed ones, progress will be forced by competition upon the others—not because the rank and file in an industry wants change. They very often do not want it. And our discontented adventurer, who if successful gets out ahead, is not burning with zeal to encourage the others to follow: he hopes they will not. But as the price of survival they do follow. They are not happy about it and neither is he. It is a fiendishly clever system to force people to rise above themselves—to get progress out of essentially unprogressive people.

We see from the above that the economic problem is a very complicated one. But in fact it is being solved day by day, ordinarily without much fanfare nor without arousing the admiration of most of the people who have come to take it for granted. To appreciate the importance of this system let us imagine that a "man from Mars" had come to our planet. He had been shown the various mechanical marvels that we have and he has had the chance to see the whole population of the United States producing goods and services and consuming them. He might have observed the various parts of the economic problem as has been outlined above. It is very likely that if he had contemplated all these things, he would be amazed at the system which accomplished all this and his most natural question would be "Who is the boss?" When he was told that no one was the boss, but that this was a system which worked more or less automatically, at least without the decision of any consciously selected group or board or bureaucracy, he might well say that this is the greatest marvel of all, far surpassing our mechanical and scientific advances. And I think soberly we can say that considering the breadth of this problem, not only in one country but in the relationships of people of different countries and all of the people of the world, that the development of this system of divison of labor, exchange, prices, competition, and its other aspects warrants our earlier comment. It does indeed constitute the greatest social achievement that the human race has made.

VII.

THE DISCIPLINE OF THE MARKET

In the light of these functions which must be performed by any successful economic system, one might sympathize with the man from Mars who felt that surely there must be a conscious control. Of course, some societies in the world are theoretically organized on that basis, although even those find that there are limits to the possible degree of detailed control. But, for us, the serious objection to resorting to that device is that it would defeat the chief social end, which is to enable individuals to advance their own intellectual, spiritual, recreational, and economic ends. To approach this ideal, individuals must be free to be good or bad, wise or foolish, to produce more or less as they see fit, to work or to loaf and to work at those particular things which they may choose.

There can never be a perfect reconciliation of two such conflicting basic demands. The modern democratic-capitalistic solution is to make it attractive through prices (wages, profits, interests, and rents), prestige, and social approval for people to do those things which the society wants done, and at the same time to allow the individuals freedom to do otherwise if they so choose.

This is the incentives aspect of our system. If the society needs more engineers, the rewards of an engineering career, both in monetary and prestige terms, will be increased for the simple reason that value attaches to those items which are desired and scarce. In response to these rewards, more young men will tend to choose this field; and when there are too many of them, opposite forces will nudge them more or less forcibly into other lines. Insofar as this system works satisfactorily, it is unnecessary for anyone to issue orders for people to go into this field or to impose prohibitions against going into that.

The relation of this kind of an economic system to the ideal of a free society can be stated in various ways. One of them is that this is about the only possible system which can provide the necessary degree of discipline and which can also be free in the sense that individuals have a high degree of freedom as to what they are going to do and how they are going to live. Another relationship between the two is that the incentives system will only work satisfactorily if there is a free and relatively unfettered market. In this system, prices, wages, interests, rents, and profits are indicators or parts of the control mechanism which regulates the economy. If goods and services are scarce, their prices of them should be high. This serves as an inducement for people to produce these products and as an inducement to the consumers to conserve and economize on them as long as they are scarce. So also, if the system is working, the demand for labor in one part of the country will reflect itself in higher wages in that part of the country, which are supposed to attract workers to it. Likewise, a shift of labor between occupations is effected. In the matter of allocation of resources: if capital is needed in one part of the country, this will reflect itself in higher interest rates, which attracts the desired capital. The higher interest rates will also preclude or discourage the use of this scarce resource for less important uses. Or, if there is a shortage of housing, it would be expected that rents and selling prices of houses would go up. This acts as a stimulus to house building and to a correction of the observed shortage.

A requirement of an effective free market system is that it must be so set up and the rules of the game and the surrounding conditions so established as to make it profitable for people individually to do what they collectively need to have done. To a greater degree than the dictators recognized some years ago, this is a requirement for any society. The totalitarian state only runs into it in a less sharp and definite way. One illustration among many is the social value of a stable currency. On the whole, individuals prompted by their own self interest are more likely to follow a socially desirable course in the presence of a stable currency than under the expectation of unstable money and prices.

An apocryphal story illustrating this point was told in the years following World War I when Austria had gone through a most severe inflation. There were two brothers in Austria. One of them was a veritable model of thrift, industry, and foresightedness. He worked consistently and saved part of his earnings, looking to provision against contingencies and the needs of his old age. The other was something of a rake and incidentally he indulged himself in champagne parties with attractive young women. Incidental to these parties, he adopted the pleasant and sentimental custom of saving the champagne corks and putting the date and the initials of the girl on each cork as mementoes. By the time of the postwar period he had saved several bushels of these corks. Then came the inflation. He was able to sell the champagne corks for more than his brother's bank account and investments were worth.

This anecdote may only serve to point a cynical moral that "virtue is its own and its only reward." But looking at it more seriously, it appears that society had allowed to develop an instability of the currency which made it unprofitable for individuals to do those things which society needed to have done and profitable to act in an antisocial way.

Another example was Britain in the years following World War II. The country was plagued by its inability to buy needed goods from the outside world. The authorities in Whitehall carried on a continuous propaganda effort, urging the people to a course of thrift and self denial. The theme was "we are poor—very poor." And so they were as a nation, but because of inflation and the rising wages which the unions and the Labor government could not or would not check, the average Englishman didn't feel poor at all. He had the tangible evidence of money in his pocket. The national need and individual motivation were at loggerheads. A free market incentives system, with a stable currency, is more likely to avoid these conflicts.

Of course, if the acts in question are sufficiently antisocial we will pass laws against them, as for example laws against stealing, fraud, and such. But for the most part a free society has to depend upon the attractiveness of doing things which the society needs to have done, and not upon punishment for failing to do them.

VIII.

WEAKENING OF DISCIPLINE

Proposals of Consumers and Workers

The problem in a free society is that there are always some people who do not want to conform to the discipline which is necessary for its successful operation. And there are various ways in which they can thwart the disciplinary forces. Take, for example, the free market way of overcoming regional unemployment. The system left to itself would produce lower wages in that part of the country suffering from that affliction on the simple basis that the supply of labor greatly exceeds the demand. But it has become an accepted principle of most labor unions that wage rates ought to be the same throughout the country. It may be that what that area of unemployment needs most of all is a higher degree of industrialization. The low wages which a free market would produce would make it attractive for industrialists to move into that area and in the course of time the increased industrialization would raise the wages as well as provide the needed jobs.

The nonindustrial areas of the South have long suffered from inadequate employment opportunities in relation to the industrial areas of the North. Wages have in fact been lower in the South and this has encouraged the migration of industries or still better the growth of them in the South. This beneficent effect has provided jobs and has raised wages. Insofar as this has happened, the free market system is working as it should.

But when workers of the North see the plants moving away from their area into the South their natural reaction, and often a successful one, is to establish a higher wage in the South by minimum wage laws or by pressure of unions in the South, which will make it unattractive for the industrialists to make this move. Naturally, if this succeeds, the movement to industrialization of the South would be retarded, which was what the Northern workers wanted. One might ask: "If advancing wages by natural forces is good, why isn't the planned advance by coercion of government or union also good?" The reason is that the higher wage induced by increased demand for labor will be proportionate to increased productivity, the other kind is proportionate to the political or union power exerted. High wages are no obstacle to the movement of industry into an area, if the high wage is based on high productivity. But the use of non-market power to level out wages in a county represents a weakening of the regulatory influence of the market system.

Another and related attitude toward geographic mobility of labor is in the dislike of workers to move to places where there is a demand for labor. The newer idea is that employment-making institutions should be brought to the worker, not vice versa. The growth of this concept has a bearing on our perennial problem of unemployment. We can for long periods have labor shortages in one part of the country and a surplus of labor in other parts. The standard wage and the resistance to moving to the job are examples of forces that reduce the mobility, i.e., freedom and flexibility of the market. The relation to a free society is that, insofar as such departures from a free market have their logical effect, the necessity (or excuse) for extended government action is increased. If artificially high wages in a backward area slow down the growth of industry, we will see more of area subsidies in which the government tries to do what the free market is not allowed to do. Likewise with the resistance to geographic mobility of labor, the government may have to step in to start and operate industries at places where the workers are.[1]

Likewise, in the matter of rents, with the shortage of housing developed by the war the natural and, from the point of view of the whole society, the desirable result was to raise rents. The higher rents would have two effects, one to increase the supply of housing and thus to remedy the basic cause of the problem, and the other to induce people to "double up," thus for the time being "making do" with the amount of housing that was actually available.[2] But, of course, there is strong opposition to these by tenants and, tenants seem nowadays to have more political influence than landlords. The former was felt to represent human rights and the latter property rights, though it is a bit difficult to see why the landlord is less human than the tenant. At any rate, rent controls were established. This had the effect of benefiting the people who had some prior claim on houses but it was quite unfortunate for those who were returning from military service or for other reasons were desiring to move into communities.

This favoring of those who are "in" is incidentally a common characteristic of government orders which displace the free market. The rent case is but one example of a very general but rarely discussed principle of government action. It is that the "ins" are generally favored over the newcomers, the outsiders. The reasons are clear in this case. First, the vociferous ones were those who were occupying the existing facilities and whose landlords wanted to raise their rents, while those excluded were a less identifiable group. Second, long-standing rental rates had gained some aura of "fairness," and the threatened increase was regarded as a departure from normal. Third, the immediate and most apparent result of free market forces would be to increase the returns of the landlords at the expense of tenants, even though the landlords' costs of maintenance, taxes, insurance, etc., had risen substantially. Perhaps this was regarded as socially bad because it was felt that the former were "better off" than the latter—a proposition that

[1] I observed an example in Sweden where the government established a steel plant in the north to give employment to men who live there, although it was generally conceded that this was not an economical place for the plant. Costs were inevitably high. Because steel costs were high the product could only be sold competitively in Sweden at a loss. A high price would make the plan viable but this could only be maintained by an import tariff to prevent the competition of foreign steel. When conditions of a free market deteriorate the area of government action increases. Satisfying the desires of the people of the north to have work brought to them resulted in a loss of freedom to all the consumers of steel products to buy where they pleased.

[2] It must be conceded that in the particular postwar situation the usual effect on construction and, thus the supply of housing, would probably have been held in check by shortages of labor and materials. The other effect—"doubling up"—would be present in full force.

would require many exceptions in the form of widows or married couples who were renting the family homes. At any rate the income of the landlord was popularly viewed as "unearned," being a return on capital, while the other was regarded as "earned." The ideological case in favor of the established tenant is apparently very strong in the mind of the voters.

There are only two illustrations of the possibility and the inclination of using noneconomic forces to thwart the action of the market. Naturally, if these things are done, the market system will not function well, any more than a thermostatic control system would function well if the householder persists in applying hot water bottles or ice packs to the thermometer. When the system, hampered in this way, does not function well, then the argument will be advanced that it is quite obvious that free enterprise has failed and, therefore, the state must step in to build the houses or to provide subsidies for doing so. The interference with the functioning of the free market creates a situation in which there is apparent need for still further interference and so the process becomes cumulative. So much so that in France the repercussions of the rent controls started after World War I were still felt after 40 years in a continued housing shortage and in the inequity of high rents on new buildings and unreasonably low rents on old ones. Again, the established tenants are protected as against others in the economy including especially the newcomers to the rental market.

Obstacles by Businessmen

The illustrations that have been given are of interferences requested by the consumers or by the workers. However, the number of requests for interference with the working of the competitive market is also considerable from the business group. This is ironical, because businessmen generally in this country give strong endorsement to the free enterprise system, but on many occasions they are the very ones who demand such interferences as would prevent the system from working. Indeed, the object of the proposed interferences is quite definitely to prevent the working of the system in their particular case. The classic example of this is protective tariffs, in which the businessmen of one country try to protect themselves against the competition of those from another country.

Another quite popular one is the demand for so called fair trade laws. These are thinly disguised devices for protecting the "regular" dealers from competition with cut-rate stores, discount houses, and other marketing innovators. On the face of it the proposal seems to be to allow a manufacturer to set the resale prices on products which he has manufactured. The demands for such laws, however, do not come so much from the manufacturers as they do from the retailers. The point seems to be that the retailers themselves could not, by agreement, maintain a price. But if the power to fix the price is conferred upon the manufacturer by law, then the retailers can demand, with threat of boycott, that the manufacturer should exercise this power and set a single price for all retailers. Thus will the power of government and the manufacturers accomplish the result which the retailers could not have accomplished through their own collusion.

The many forms of licensing and the interferences with interstate traffic brought about by the demand of various business groups are further illustrations of the fact that these proposed interferences with the functioning of the free market system do not rise solely from those who dislike the market system. They lead one to wonder whether the free market system is more seriously threatened by its friends or by its enemies. These few illustrations suggest that a free society must be based upon a free market. A free market requires that prices, wages, and the other rewards shall be free to rise or fall in response to the varying conditions of demand for the product or service and the factors controlling the supply of them.

It will be noted that the interferences that have been described have all relied upon group action. These may be either groups that are encouraged, strengthened or at least permitted to exist by the government or it may be the government itself. Those who adhere to the philosophy of a free society are, therefore, likely to be opposed to powerful groups of whatever functional sort—workers, retailers, manufacturers, bankers, or others. And they are equally suspicious of measures undertaken by the government on behalf of the special groups. Developments along both of these lines have proceeded sufficiently in recent decades to give cause for concern about the future of a free system. On the one side there has been the permissive and encouraging legislation for the legal recognition of functional groups such as labor unions, farm blocs, and professional associations, and on the other hand the use of government (local, state, and national) for conferring benefits upon particular groups. These suggest that a free market could hardly have developed in the absence of a democratic political system; but the question now arises whether the free market, capitalist system can continue in the presence of this kind of a political system. In other words the market and economic freedom, which were encouraged by a government of limited powers, can very well give way to a market control sponsored by the people themselves. They are often inclined to disregard the proper limits in government power when it is found that the power can be used for their special group advantages. This is a point to which we will revert later, but it suggests a fallacy in the idea that you do not need to fear the power of government as long as it is your own government.

The people who demand and often get these special favors, which have the effect of weakening the free enterprise system, are for the most part not people who are opposed to the system as a whole. They are often quite vocal advocates of rugged individualism, Americanism, free enterprise, and competition. They merely wish to get some special dispensations, not to overthrow the system. This is not a very admirable characteristic of human nature but it is quite common. People generally think in terms of special cases, not of large classes or general principles. To praise free enterprise and to say that competition is the life of trade is one thing. But to accept those "sneaky fellows" who cut their costs and then cut prices as the personal embodiment of this competitive principle is quite another. If we are going to maintain a free society which is always subject to the pressures of groups of citizens we must get people to think in terms of the broad, perhaps abstract, questions as well as of their own particular case. If a free people are going to preserve their free system they do need a philosophy.

Groups Who Reject Validity of Market

There is another group who would frankly deny the validity of the verdict of the market price. The market verdict is essentially a democratic one. When a product is produced and offered on the market the whole public has its chance to vote on whether it is acceptable or not and they vote quite seriously, because the ballots are their own dollars. But there are those in the community who doubt that the decision of the majority is the right decision. I had a talk some years ago with Sir William Beveridge, a leading Socialist statesman of England. The conversation turned to the plight of some sharecroppers and other poor people in the rural sections of our South. We both agreed that it was unfortunate. I suggested that the solution lay in increasing the productivity of these people so that their purchasing power would be higher and then they could live better. Sir William was not entirely in agreement with this, for he said: "But the question is even if they had larger incomes, would they spend them for the right things." From this incident and other indications it seems doubtful if Sir William really accepted the validity of the rule of the market. Certainly acceptance of that principle would imply a right of earners to spend their money as they saw fit. It was presumptuous to imply that the preferences of others should be substituted for their own.

No doubt there is ground for a feeling of depression about the shabby purchases of such people. There is no denying that there is a difference between good taste and bad taste and perhaps between wise consumption and foolish consumption. But the person of truly liberal convictions will realize that there is no quick and easy way to raise standards. The typical socialist or near socialist is quite willing to interfere to see to it that the people get the "right things." I judge from conversations with socialists in a number of countries—particularly in England, Norway, Sweden, India, and Ceylon—that "wrong" things in this context are not those that would be demonstrably harmful to others than the users, or even in a positive way to the users such as certain drugs or even allegedly of tobacco or liquor. The judgment extends to such matters as the citizen's preference between better housing and transportation. I recall asking a Swedish member of the Socialist government during their effort (1950) to conserve dollars in exchange why they singled out automobiles for special import restrictions. His reply was that "we" did not think more cars were very important for the people. Particularly he added that the young men who had cars would gain a social advantage in the eyes of the girls over those who did not and this was "unfair." When I asked who the "we" was in this case, he replied in surprise at the question that, of course, he meant the government.

I have yet to meet an unavowed socialist in any country who shrank at the responsibilities inherent in playing God. Such an attitude may be consistent with a high regard for the welfare of "the people" in the abstract, but not for the dignity and individuality of actual flesh and blood individuals. The fact that the character, tastes, and personality of this individual will not always stand very close inspection, is no doubt a reason that the socialist and his welfare state cousin are more partial to "the masses" or "the proletariat" in the abstract than they are to the individual man or woman. (Incidentally Marx showed this characteristic. For while he bemoaned the plight of the proletariat in the mass, he personally displayed no desire to share their lives. Pictures of him display a luxuriant beard, monocle, a gold-headed cane, and a Prince Albert coat. I find no evidence that he regarded himself as a buddy of the individual workingman.) The classic liberal recognizes that the state may decide though unwisely what goods will be produced and, therefore, consumed, but it cannot legislate character, tastes, and ethical standards and that these in the last analysis are what really count.

Literary people, artists, musicians, and their associates and sympathizers frequently encounter an unwillingness on the part of the public to accept their offerings. The public is likely to be conservative or indifferent in their tastes. Because progress in the arts involves change, the divergence of views between the creators and their audience seems unavoidable. But in a free market system the decisions by which men live are made by the audience. The creative ones naturally rebel against this. They find themselves in a difficult position, for they do not want to appear to be undemocratic, which they certainly would be if they frankly rejected the judgment of the masses. Many of them meet this impasse by pretending that the masses would like the same things as they, the elite, want, if only the profit seeking publishers and dealers would offer them. By some mysterious process they conclude that the wicked profit motive is better served by producing things the consumers do not want than those they do want. Thus their resentment finds an acceptable object, and this can lead to a hostile attitude toward the whole free market system.

These people of the arts do face a real problem in their efforts to introduce new things in an area where there is general resistance. I think they are in error in favoring an authoritarian answer. They make the mistake of thinking that the state or any governing board would, of course, support standards similar to their own. This is a very unreliable assumption. One thinks, for example, of the extremely conservative artistic tastes of Hitler and Stalin. No, these people might far better rely on the free market, for, while the majority may reject the new things, there will always be a select minority who will applaud. Indeed, there is a substantial number who will be inclined to applaud only because the things are new. Also there are, at least in this country, substantial funds for the support of the avant-garde provided by foundations and wealthy individuals, not on the ground of their own liking for the products, but a desire to encourage experimentation. This is an example of a slight departure from the price market test which seems well justified.

The artistic group, like many intellectuals, are hostile to the market. This is a short-sighted view, for a free market system, as the term implies, leans toward freedom and the philosophy of a free society is favorable to variety. The mass may be hostile but the essence of a free system is not the overwhelming power of the mass, but the rights of minorities, which in this case provide the opportunity for trying new forms and ideas. Historically a high development of commerce has usually been accompanied by an active cultural life. And there have usually been benefactors from the business classes. One thinks of the great banking family of the Medicis and how much they contributed to the flowering of the Renaissance, in providing financial resources and also an intelligent leadership. Lorenzo the Magnificent was the shrewd banker whose banking house was creditor to the Papacy and to several crowned heads of Europe, the realistic political power of Florence, the connoisseur of arts, and founder of the Academy devoted to the rebirth of art and philosophy. In this very important period in the history of civilization, the arts and the market place were closely allied.

There is another group which rejects the free market system. It comprises those who are frankly aristocratic in their views. They regard their standards as higher (which they possibly are) and are ready to force them on the common people who in time may come to like them. It is a little surprising to see this element showing itself in America in recent years in the persons of those who argue that in our affluent society "the people" have all they really need of necessities and a moderate degree of comfort. Hence, further income should be spent for them in the public sector where wiser heads will direct production.

These groups raise their obstacles in one way or another to the smooth working of the market.

Complexity of Modern Market

On the intellectual side there is another line or argument directed against the free enterprise system. It is particularly effective with intellectuals who are imbued with the concept of social evolution—i.e., that everything changes and that it is essential to keep up with the times. This has a popular appeal for two reasons, first that this idea of a tendency for economic institutions to evolve, as capitalism grew out of feudalism (or as a variant of the idea goes that it grew out of the decay of feudalism) was one of the more readily accepted items of Marx's doctrine. Second, the rapid change in technology which we see all around us suggests that anything old is presumed to be antiquated —as though the great truths known to the ancients and preserved to the present are to be discarded like the succeeding models of automobiles.

Specifically the argument in this vein against the market system that has received considerable support in recent years, especially since 1930 and still more specifically during the period of the great depression, is that even if these free market forces were adequate to control the economy in earlier days when conditions were much more simple, they are not adequate for the more complicated world of today. Franklin Roosevelt, particularly after he had embraced the philosophy of the planned economy, was very scornful of what he called the "horse-and-buggy age." This approach makes an appeal to certain economists who do not like utterly to desert the principles of the founder of our science, Adam Smith, and who would still like to justify a high degree of government control at the present time. It is an ingenious argument enlisting the support of people of various schools of thought and political inclinations.

In the view of this writer, however, the argument is almost completely fallacious. The merit of the automatic or semiautomatic regulation of economic affairs is that it can take care of a much more complicated system than can government control. To have a conscious control over a system as complicated as we have today would require an impossible collection of economic facts. We must bear in mind that government in this context is nothing more than a group of individuals, and that the capacity of any group of individuals to bring into their knowledge and effective control all of the millions of facts that arise in a modern economy is quite inadequate for the appalling task involved.

The merit of the natural competitive system is that under its sway it is not necessary for any individuals to possess supernatural wisdom nor to maintain an impossibly extensive range of factual knowledge. The businessman under such a system does not have to be an economist in the conduct of his daily affairs, though a knowledge of that subject may be of some aid to him as a citizen in recommending public policies. Take, for example, a situation in which there is a threatened shortage of some material, let us say tin. In a thoroughly controlled economy someone or some small group must anticipate this. They must also try to determine why we have this shortage of tin, because without this knowledge they will not know what remedial steps to take. They must then decide upon measures to be taken: how we shall ration the limited supply of tin and what we can do to increase the supply. Even for one minor product such as tin this is a major job.

Under a free system all the ordinary businessman who uses tin needs to know is that the price of tin has gone up. Actually this may have happened because of political disturbances in Bolivia or other esoteric factors very difficult for anyone to determine. Under the price system, however, the results of these facts will be registered in a rise in the price of tin and the businessman acts upon this signal. He may strive to find substitute materials and, thereby, he will conserve the limited supply of this product. In case of some raw materials he may stimulate his research people to try to find substitutes of a synthetic nature. He may simply raise the price of the finished product which contains the tin. If he does the latter he is thereby signaling to the consumers that we need to conserve our supply of this product. The consumer does not need to know why, he merely observes that the price has gone up and he does the sensible thing of being more careful in the purchase of those things that contain tin.

So these signals provided largely by price ramify throughout the whole system and people naturally do the things which the situation calls for, namely, to try to increase the supply of the product and if that is not possible then to conserve the product in which the short supply occurs. It is a far more sensitive means of adjusting to a situation than would be the studies and the subsequent decisions, directives, and allocations of a bureau in Washington.

As Professor Hayek has well put it in an essay on the "Nature and Use of Knowledge in Society,"[3] it is by this decentralized method that our society is able to draw upon that special knowledge of time and place which resides a little in the mind of each participant in the economic process and does not require the impossible condition of being centered at some one place or in the minds of some small group of people. The idea needs to be emphasized because in these modern days we have such great reliance upon science that we may be deluded into thinking that most of the decisions made in this country can be made on a scientific basis. In spite of the value of science in establishing some general truths, it is not capable of controlling efficiently the day by day actions of the people of the country.

My friend down the street who operates a gas station is not a very learned man. He would be utterly at a loss to write a book on the science and practice of gasoline delivery. But for all this, I am confident that he knows more about how to run a gas station on that particular corner for his particular clientele than does anybody else in the world. The sum total of the knowledge of all these gas station operators is the means by which the mundane job of distributing gasoline must be done. So it is with the many other activities. The requirement of a good economic system is that it must utilize and be based upon the utterly tremendous knowledge which is possessed by all of the millions of people of the United States, and which it is impossible to mobilize and codify. This is what a free economic system does.

An observation of the experience of mankind with different kinds of systems at the present and in the distant past supports this view. A high degree of control of a country or of an economy is most suited

[3] F. A. Hayek, *American Economic Review,* September 1945.

to one which is simple—not the opposite. These comparatively simple conditions characterize agricultural economies. Authoritarian methods and autocracy have been and are more commonly found in agricultural economies than in active commercial and industrial economies. The growth of industry and, even more, of commerce was a major reason for the breakdown of government controls in Europe in the seventeenth and eighteenth centuries. Adam Smith in 1776 was in a sense only spelling out the rationale of what was happening and had to happen with the growing role of trade. The elaborate controls of mercantilism had to go. They were forced out by the increasing complexity of economic life. And it was the increasingly free system of England in contrast to its own earlier state and in contrast to the continued controls on the Continent that goes far to explain England's tremendous upsurge to a position of unquestioned commercial and economic dominance in the nineteenth century. Fortunately our country, after a brief flirtation with industry codes and price fixing under the National Recovery Administration, has apparently abandoned these devices as a general mode of control. Sporadic price control measures like laws against selling below cost, "fair trade" laws, and so on, we have, but few people envisage a complete system of that kind. Occasionally the government undertakes to set the price of steel or to fix wages by only thinly-veiled devices, but this is still a fairly long step from systematic planning. The danger in this country could become real in the event of another protracted depression and, even without that, the planless hodgepodge of hindrance to the free price system is surely not helpful.

A related instance was that of the different economic systems that had grown up by 1860 between our North and South. Slavery, which is a method of authoritarian control, was reasonably effective in the South, particularly in those parts of the South in which the one crop of cotton dominated. But slavery was completely unfitted as a method of organization of labor in the North where the conditions were made more complicated by new methods of manufacture and commerce.

One is tempted to say too that the system of autocracy and centralized control was more feasible in Russia when the country was primarily agricultural and that it will become less and less feasible as the country gains a more highly developed industry and commerce. The internal changes within the Russian system itself in the last few years seem to be consistent with this thesis. The proposition simply is that as the principle of division of labor is carried to higher and higher degrees and the complexity of the system increases, the necessity for relying on the special knowledge of time and place which is to be found in an individualistic society becomes greater.

This, of course, is not to say that the particular methods of organization or the particular laws existing in the nineteenth century are equally applicable in the twentieth century. There is that small degree of truth in the scornful dismissal of the horse-and-buggy age. But the basic principle that government should confine itself to those measures which are necessary to facilitate the working of a free system is just as important today as it was then and, if the argument of the above paragraphs is correct, even more important.

Thus, paradoxical as it may seem, the increasing specialization, division of labor, and extension of markets really require not more control, but a high and increasing degree of freedom of individuals to seek their own ends in ways that may seem most profitable to them.

Indeed, as we now look back upon the last two centuries, it appears that such freedom of action and of choice was an essential requirement for the creation of free markets and that they, in turn, were a prerequisite to the Industrial Revolution itself. If it is true that the Industrial Revolution depended in the first instance upon the breaking down of controls, it may well be that its extension today requires even more of that freedom. Thus, as society becomes more complex and interdependent, we will need more of that flexibility which is provided by the spontaneous aspirations and decisions of individuals, guided by the checks and balances of a free market. The feasibility of centralized planning and direction of the affairs of individuals will decline. If this be true, as we argue that it is, it suggests an escape from the hard choice between the requirements for abundance on the one side and freedom of individuals on the other. It suggests that the abundance and real security, too, are to be best attained by an extension of freedom and thus that these ideals are to be gained together—not one at the expense of the other. It gives a basis of hope that this central problem of a free society, i.e., reconciliation of interdependence and freedom, can, with wisdom and good will, be solved.

IX.

LIBERALISM—CLASSIC AND MODERN

A discussion of the philosophy of a free society is complicated by the fact that some terms which naturally arise in such a discussion are poorly defined. Particularly this is true of the term "liberal." If one were writing at an earlier time, or if one now were writing primarily for a European audience, the title of this essay might be "The Liberal Philosophy." The term liberal and also liberalism was at one time and is today in some places well understood. The central idea of this philosophy is individualism. It calls for restricted government and has other characteristics which were well recognized and understood.

However, today the term in popular usage in the United States has come to have an almost opposite meaning. It now characteristically implies extended powers of government and an emphasis upon the needs of the society or of groups in the society, and a correspondingly restricted importance of the individual. Why this transition of meaning has taken place is not entirely clear. The new popular meaning may have derived from liberal in the sense of a broadly permissive interpretation of the powers of government under our Constitution. The term has in fact been used in that way to characterize certain judges or decisions of the Supreme Court. This, of course, reverses the older meaning, for that meaning implied *limitations* on the power of government and corresponding liberalization or expansion of the liberty (freedom) of the individual. And there may have been other more or less logical reasons for the reversal of the old meaning.

One suspects, however, that the reversal primarily reflects a conscious or unconscious use of the art of semantics, for the term "liberal" is a "good term" or at least it used to be. But since it has had a pleasant connotation, people of quite opposing philosophies have tried to seize upon it. The consequence is that the term in America today seems to identify a position close to but not quite as far "left" as socialism. This sense of "near socialist" reverses the earlier meaning. The new meaning is thus not in my opinion a natural outgrowth of the old meaning. Some writers imply that it is just this—that the old fashioned liberalism merely adapted itself to changing conditions and that there has been an unbroken continuance of the liberal idea from Jeffersonian democracy to populism to the New Deal, the Square Deal, and the New Frontier and the War on Poverty. This does not stand scrutiny. The one outstanding tenet of the recent "deals" is expanded power of centralized government and direct action for the welfare of the people. The old liberalism of the Founding Fathers was a philosophy of carefully localized and restricted government and expanded opportunity for citizens to seek their own welfare. The old and new concepts are opposites.

The confusion is compounded when the term "conservative" is used as the opposite of liberal. The terms "progressive," "radical," and "reactionary," are also ambiguous. The difficulty in part arises because there are two different *bases* of comparing social philosophies and consequently two dichotomies. First, philosophies may differ as to relative emphasis placed on the individual or the group. This is the question of man vs. society and it provides one basic classification of social ideas. In classic usage the liberal philosophy was identified with the individual and his defense against the state or other group. We may occasionally refer to this philosophy as classic liberalism. The socialist (in a broad sense of this term) emphasized the group—usually the state. So the opposition was: liberal vs. socialist. A second dichotomy turns on the question of relative emphasis given to tradition, history, the lessons of the past, on the one side, or to sheer rationality or impulse of the present on the other. In this classification a conservative is one who attaches great importance to the continuity of social developments, the lessons of the past, to the "wisdom of the race." He would "conserve" established values. He assumes that the presumption is in favor of the existing methods and that the burden of proof for any proposed change rests upon the reformer. He admits that changes (reforms) will be needed, but they should come gradually. His opposite is the progressive. He relies on the intelligence and ingenuity of men at any time to tackle afresh the problems of the day. He is likely to refer approvingly to "this brave new world" and to be greatly impressed by the products of recent researches and the values of modern science. This progressive view was carried to its extreme at the time of the French Revolution when the religious statues were destroyed and people were asked to place their reliance on the Goddess of Reason. Indeed the philosophical forerunner of the revolution was the Age of Enlightenment where old values and guideposts were swept away. A reaction to these extremes was provided by Edmund Burke who gave perhaps the best defense of conservatism and, along with John Adams, stands among the patron saints of the thoughtful conservative. The distinction is obviously worth making for the relative emphasis upon the lessons of the past and upon the sheer rationality of the present will always properly be present in the discussion of social questions. But only confusion results when we fail to recognize the different bases for comparison.

Now it is apparent that the former dichotomy of individual vs. the group and the latter of tradition vs. sheer rationality are quite independent of one another. It is quite conceivable, for example, that the classic liberal will defend his views of individual rights by an appeal to tradition and he will often speak of ancient and well-established rights. In this case he will be attempting to preserve (conserve) the liberal society as he sees it against those who would emasculate it in the name of reform. In this case it is quite apparent that "liberal" and "conservative" are not true opposites. Instead the liberal is also a conservative. The use of the terms as opposites leads to grave confusion of thought.

A simple analogy may illustrate the futile results of mixing dichotomies. If a farmer were to send his helper into the orchard with instructions to put the sweet apples into one basket and the red apples into another, the assistant could be excused for being puzzled. It is quite possible to separate apples as to red and yellow *or* as to sweet and sour, but it is not logically possible to separate them as to sweet and red, for one is not the opposite of the other. This is what people are trying to do when they contrast conservative and liberal. The terms refer to two different bases of classification. We can set up the two dichotomies and the corresponding ideologies as follows:

First Basis of Classification

Emphasis on the groups	vs.	Emphasis on the individual
Related ideologies:		Related ideologies:
communism, fascism, socialism	vs.	individualism, classic liberalism, anarchy

Second Basis of Classification

Emphasis on pure reason	vs.	Emphasis on tradition and experience
Related ideologies:		Related ideologies:
progressivism, radicalism	vs.	conservatism, reaction

The opposite of a socialist is a liberal; the opposite of a progressive is a conservative. We will not stop here to comment on the several views held by these groups. We might mention, however, that the terms used by the adherents of the several groups to describe themselves are quite different from the terms their opponents use to describe them. For example, those in the right-hand column in the first classification will use such terms about themselves as upstanding individualists and self-reliant. About their opponents they will use such terms as autocracy, enslavement of the masses, dictatorship, regimentation, beehive system, and "Reds."

Those on the other side of this dichotomy will speak of their own system as "peoples democracy," "pure democracy," the "larger freedom," "victory of the masses." If they represent one of the more moderate variants of the collectivist persuasions found in Western countries they will be the "defenders of the poor" against the "malefactors of great wealth" and of the "underprivileged" which used to mean "poor" but now means anyone who is less well off in any respect. So the uneducated have recently become the "culturally underprivileged." Needless to say these self-styled liberals are for the "common man," at least in the mass. Their opposites will be "selfish individualists" and "heartless defenders of property rights against human rights."

The progressives have their own terms for themselves and some very choice epithets for the conservatives. Speaking of themselves they are "forward looking," "progressive," "adaptable," "practical" with not much use for theories. Their opponents will be called "unimaginative," "tradition bound," "stick-in-the-muds," "stand patters," "moss backs," "reactionaries," "hang-overs of the horse-and-buggy age." (They will not often refer to them as "conservatives" for, so far at least, that is not a really bad word.) The conservatives will return the compliments with such expressions as "fuzzy headed," "soft headed," "wild eyed," iconoclasts, "rockers of the boat," "upsetters of the apple cart," "never met a pay roll," and other reflections on their common sense. They are not likely to call them progressive for that too is a good word; at least, no one wants to admit that he is unprogressive.

All this is mildly amusing, but if as some say we think in words, this jargon is not conducive to clarity. People invent more and more colorful terms of disapproval of their opponents than they do of approval of their own ideology.

Faced by this confusion, a liberal in the classic sense of the term has the choice of trying to reform the popular usage by bringing people back to the original and logical concept of liberalism, or to accept the debasement of the language as a *fait accompli* and seek other terms to express himself. The latter seems to be the only feasible policy. Since it seems more realistic to accept the popular use of the word liberal, those of the writer's persuasion must find some other term to describe our ideas. Occasionally, however, we hope that we may be excused for reverting to the good old term of classic liberalism to describe our own ideology.

We have chosen to speak of the "philosophy of a free society." We may be accused of a semantic trick in that "free" is a "good" word and thus creates an unfair bias toward things so described. But there is a logical defense. A system that glorifies and extends the power of government does not deserve to be called "free," because the essence of government and the one attribute that it possesses above the other institutions of mankind is the power of coercion. Since coercion and freedom are opposed, a system that minimizes the reliance upon government and coercion of any kind can logically be called a free system and its opposite a controlled or planned or directed system. And the propriety of these terms does not depend on whether the government derives its power from the consent of the governed or from a dictatorship or whether the government is activated by good motives or bad.

Coercion or free choice—these are the significant alternatives in considering whether a society is free or controlled, even though we must recognize that neither is likely to be found in its pure form. Coercion, of course, is required in our society for deterring would-be criminals and for some other purposes. The philosophy of a free society only requires that these instances be kept at a minimum.

The term "liberalism" has been given little attention in current writing or talk. In daily use we speak of men as liberals or of liberal ideas or liberal plans. But is it not surprising that we have few or no serious exposition of the general philosophy of present-day liberalism? The term is used in the concrete but not much in the abstract. One explanation is that there is no rounded philosophy, but rather that the term covers almost any reform that is inspired by a desire to help some unfortunate group and which involves use of the power of the state. The late Henry Simons once wrote that any economist who would attempt to improve the lot of labor by encouraging occupational groups (labor unions) was morally bound to consider what would be the effect on society if all functional groups became organized and used similar tactics to advance their ends. This would require a general picture of society under a regime of powerful groups. No notable book of this kind comes to mind.

The same cannot be said about liberalism in the classic sense. There are many. One of these would be Lippmann's *The Good Society*. Another would be Hayek's *Road to Serfdom* and his *Constitution of Liberty*. There are several writings of Von Mises, e.g., *Human Action* and Roepke's *The Humane Society* not to mention such older classics as Mill's *Essay on Liberty*.

Also in the dichotomy of progressive vs. conservative we have little well-reasoned defense of the former but several of the latter. There are, for example, the scholarly *The Conservative Mind* by Russell Kirk, and Rossiter's *Conservatism in America*.

The writer found himself a few years ago engaged in a discussion which soon turned into a debate before a college audience with a certain well known Harvard professor on Economic Planning vs. Free Enterprise. Our arguments did not really meet, for my opponent announced at the outset that we were not going to waste our time on philosophy and theories but would consider practical questions such as what are you going to do about the farm problem or about the unemployed coal miners, etc. I replied that the professor could use his time as he pleased, but I *was* going to talk about the basic principles or logic of a good society. I suspect that a more or less plausible case could have been made for the individual measures he defended, but that if that case were logically rounded and complete it would, in fact, be a defense of socialism. This he wanted to avoid. An intellectually consistent case can and has been made for socialism or for a free market system but the midway position seems to be a haphazard mixture of opposed ideas which may work reasonably well on an *ad hoc* basis for particular problems but that are virtually impossible to blend into a logically consistent philosophy that has general applicability and which can serve as a guide to long-range policy.

X.

ELEMENTS OF CLASSIC LIBERALISM

What, then, is the meaning of liberalism in this traditional sense? As a broad philosophic concept it involves, first, the view that the individual is the end and the center of our world and that human institutions are but means to advance the interests and the development of those individuals. The implication of this concept is that liberty, as a political ideal, is not a means to an end; but, as Lord Acton expressed it, "Liberty is itself the highest political end."

If we regard the whole world or even the European area, this idea of the primacy of the individual has by no means been commonplace, and it never has been universally accepted. It was opposed by the concepts of the organic nature of the state and of society, in which the individual was regarded as a means for strengthening and glorifying those groups. Against this beehive philosophy the doctrine of the prime significance of the individual is diametrically opposed.

Not only are there historical illustrations of this group philosophy, but it is only too painfully clear that these philosophies do not die easily. We have recently seen in certain countries of the world a revival of the extreme view. It was expressed by Mussolini in the slogan "Nothing outside of the state and nothing against the state" and by the injunction that was impressed upon his people to "believe, obey, and fight." Nor does one have to turn to such extremists, for in many instances in England, and some in the United States, the demands of "general welfare," "social good," and other modern terms with the same import are placed well above the liberties of individuals. Thus it is clear that an assertion of the central position of the individual about 175 years ago was a new idea and that its reassertion today is far from the platitude that it is sometimes considered to be.

Individualism

Because of this emphasis upon the individual, the doctrine of liberalism is sometimes identified as "individualism." The term does, indeed, describe one important facet of this philosophy. It is an individual philosophy in the sense just indicated, that the economic and spiritual well-being of individuals is accepted as the goal. According to it, the actual devices or social forces must, in the last analysis, be judged by their effects on individuals and upon their moral and intellectual stature.

Another aspect of individualism is the inherent conviction in each person that justice requires he should reap where he has sown; that his own welfare should in justice depend upon his own efforts, sacrifices, and foresight; and that all he has a *right* to demand of society is opportunity to seek his welfare on those terms. As a practical matter this leads to the demand for equal opportunity, the most justifiable of the demands of the "underprivileged." It is true, and fortunately so, that we do not apply this standard of self reliance and reward in its extreme form to others, for it would be a harsh world if justice were not often tempered by generosity. But to recognize and to act upon this important fact does not require an abandonment of the inner conviction that the major responsibility for a person's own welfare rests with himself. Thus one aspect of individualism and of the liberal philosophy is self-reliance, which incidentally provides a sound basis of self-respect.

The term "individualism" has, however, acquired a bad odor in some quarters, because it has been given the meaning of selfishness. That connotation is erroneous if selfishness is taken in its usual sense, for the doctrine merely implies that individuals shall be allowed to seek ends which to them appear good. Those ends can be completely generous if the individual is so inclined. It should be remembered that the greatest philanthropic enterprises, as supported both by the rich and by the masses of the people, have in this country been individualistic in the sense that individuals contributed to them or not, as they saw fit. This is the highest form of generosity. Indeed, it is the only true form of generosity. A person cannot be truly moral unless he has the freedom to be immoral, and he cannot be truly generous unless he has the freedom to be narrowly selfish. The contributions which the people of this country have freely made over and over through the Red Cross and similar organizations stand as a reply to those who would picture individualism as being merely crass materialism and money grubbing and selfishness.

According to this view government grants-in-aid leave much to be desired as expressions of generosity. For an essential principle of government is coercion. And most government projects involve application of the taxing power to all the people for purposes that seem good to some of them. There are some cases in which the voluntary feature is present in an unusual degree but they are decidedly the exception. One of these is the young people who go into the Peace Corps voluntarily. To a considerable extent their role can be described as individually generous.

This is not to say that coercion may not in some of these cases be justified as a matter of wise public policy. It is intended to suggest that the moral issue involves the decisions of individuals for their own actions and particularly their own sacrifices, not the decisions of some people, even a majority, for actions which are to be required of others.

A philosophy of individualism, far from implying selfishness provides the necessary basis not only for generosity but for all the social virtues. No man is proven to be a good man unless he has faced the choice between the right and wrong, the good and the evil. This is in a way the most important reason for freedom.

Perhaps this is the reason that God, who we are told is omnipotent, permits Satan to exist. In the Book of Job, God offered to Satan who was skeptical of the existence of a good man, the freedom to tempt "my servant Job." Obviously Job had to be free to be evil in order to be proven good.

Belief in Decency of People

The doctrine of individualism implies a belief (or faith) in the inherent decency of persons. How often individuals look in puzzlement at the clash of nations, the disputes of capital and labor, and all the other turmoil and grasping for self-interest in the world today. How often the common man says that, if he could sit down with an individual foreigner or with his boss and "talk it out," they could surely arrive at some solution of their differences. Such an attitude implies a faith in the basic decency of most people. This instinctive feeling of common people contains much truth and expresses an aspect of individualism. But if the world becomes more and more organized and if more of its affairs are handled by groups, this naturally beneficent force has little chance to operate. The golden rule, one must remember, was offered as a guide for individuals; it is highly personal. Its hope of fulfillment rests upon the assumption that the responsibilities of individuals are not to be shifted to states, unions, employers' associations, political blocs, or other centers of authority.

This faith in the decency of people is, however, tempered by another basic idea about men. It is that man is neither an angel nor is he a beast. The efforts of some to deal with him as one or the other leads to disaster. The liberal view is that everyone has his better nature and his base nature. Education, example, and his own experience under a favorable (i.e., a free) environment may improve him. It is not the best role of government to force his decisions but to give him freedom. It is also apparent that against some of his worse actions the power of government must be used to restrain. But always we should strive to work with the better nature of men, not to provide substitutes for it. As a homely expression goes: A wise carpenter works with the grain of the wood—not against it.

Rationality

The other philosophic basis of classic liberalism is a belief in the rationality of men. This belief implies, on the one side, that men are individually the best judges of their own welfare and that they are quite competent to handle their own affairs. On the other side, it implies that through free and reasonable discussion they can determine and mold their political institutions: they are not mere chips on some overwhelming "wave of the future." It was on this latter point, incidentally, that Karl Marx and the other "scientific" socialists stood in sharpest opposition to the nineteenth century liberals. The latter believed that men could through reason settle on forms of government and other institutions, while the Marxians believed that new social institutions followed old ones as ineluctably as the processes of biological evolution or the movement of a glacier. They also believed in the inevitability of the class struggle as long as capitalism remained. That particular belief, however, seems less significant than their general view of inevitability in human affairs. This belief in inevitability has had a revival in recent decades, favored no doubt by certain specific trends toward collectivism and by the growing tendency to see evolutionary trends in social affairs.

From a denial or minimizing of the rationality of men flow two alternative conclusions. First, if men are essentially stubborn and unreasonable, one may conclude that reforms and redress of grievances must be and have been accomplished only by force. This conclusion leads to placing reliance for social change upon revolution and to explaining past changes as the fruits of revolution. The second possible conclusion is that the changes which the world has made were the inevitable products of social forces which no one or no group could control. It is interesting to observe that orthodox socialism tries to ride both these horses at once. In most of Marx's writing, the latter theme of inevitability was emphasized. He says that capitalism grew out of and succeeded feudalism; it has done a good job; but it cannot last, for certain inherent forces will lead to its demise; and the succession of socialism must occur as surely as capitalism had to succeed feudalism. Socialism will emerge from the womb of capitalism. When writing in this vein, Marx does not berate capitalists, for they are helpless to avoid the natural course of events. At other times, as for example in *The Communist Manifesto* (joint authorship with Engels), Marx's invective is bitter, and he calls for the workers of the world to arise and strike down their oppressors. Here is an obvious inconsistency. If the new world is bound to come anyway, what is all the shooting about? But while there is an inconsistency, it is not so hard to understand when we recognize that both force and inevitability are negative reactions to the liberal's claim of the rationality of men. Force and inevitability are both a denial of free decisions.

Many Americans are baffled because they cannot "understand" the Russians. But is that surprising if one people starts with the premise that men are essentially rational, i.e., reasonable, while the other denies that premise? The one will rely upon logic and open discussion. The other will rely upon either physical force or the force of evolution. It would appear then that the American professors and other intellectuals, who—with great show of scientific objectivity—lay stress upon inevitable trends to which we should adapt ourselves because we cannot control them, are more closely allied to the violent, direct-action Communists than is sometimes assumed and than these intellectuals would like to admit. They agree, at least, in repudiating one of the basic premises of liberalism.

Is it not significant that the symbol of communism, which is the very antithesis of liberalism, is the clenched fist? How revealing that is! It is the universal symbol of force. It is the negation of reason. One cannot conceive of that gesture being used to accompany the invitation, "Come, let us reason together." But that invitation has, from Socrates to our time, expressed an essential aspect of the liberal philosophy.

XI.

APPLICATIONS OF CLASSIC LIBERALISM

On the side of practical policy, the philosophy of liberalism has shown itself in several ways.

Civil Liberties

One of these was in the establishment of civil and political liberties, including freedom of speech, freedom of religion, freedom of the press, freedom of assembly, and protection against arbitrary arrest. If these civil liberties appear to the present-day reader to be obvious and self-evident, that is itself evidence that he has forgotten the long centuries in which they did not exist and the fact that they came to us as the result of the bold thinking and struggles of our forefathers in the not-too-distant past; it is also evidence that he has forgotten in how many countries these freedoms which we take for granted are today denied. It is dangerous, indeed, for a people to take for granted those blessings which are not free goods and which do not exist in the nature of things. In fact, these liberties are highly artificial in the sense that they are a product of conscious thought and effort and that they would not exist in a state of nature, as indicated by the fact that they do not exist among primitive people.

Jean Jacques Rousseau was surely wrong when he argued that men in a state of nature were free and that it was civilization which placed them "everywhere in chains." No, freedom is the highly refined product of civilization. To maintain it in view of the high degree of interdependence of modern society and the need for cooperation requires, not only good will, but intelligent regard for the practical requirements of such a system. That is to say it calls for both resolution to maintain eternal vigilance, as our forefathers maintained, but also for a high degree of genuine statecraft. The latter is a commodity which is not overabundant and is showing no signs of increasing with the need for it.

Minorities

A second expression of the philosophy of liberalism is in the rights of minorities. This particular aspect of liberalism is very popular today, at least as it applies to racial and religious groups. But every individual is a minority in one way or another and thus the only firm basis for the rights of minorities of any kind or classification is in the rights of the individual. The important minority to keep our eyes on is the minority of one. This fact can well be considered by leaders of the Civil Rights movement today.

Also in the philosophy of liberalism, the rights of minorities must stand as firmly against the will of a majority as they stand against the will of a dictator. The essential question is not who exercises the power, but whether the rights of a minority, no matter how small, against a majority, no matter how great or powerful, are to be recognized and respected. To some, this aspect of liberalism is the most significant one.

It is also one that requires careful thought. The rights of individuals like those of the state must be defined and limited. The man whose house stands in the way of a transcontinental highway will find that his private property rights are not unlimited. The principle of eminent domain will prevail in this case. Here is a case where the requirements of society are regarded as sufficient to override the private property right. This has to be. But it should be noted that the decision had to be against the individual because of the degree of the inconvenience to the society, not because of the size of the majority that wanted to seize his land. The degree of inconvenience would be very great, because if private property rights of all owners were to be made absolute such a highway or a railroad could not be built, for almost certainly some individual would be obdurate. So the most we can say is that such a limitation on private property should be made only when no reasonable alternative can be found and it should not depend upon the number of people who clamor for it, but upon the seriousness of the clash of private and public interest and that it should always be governed by due process of law.

Minimizing Authority

The two basic elements of the liberal idea—emphasis upon the individual human being and the belief in the rationality of men—lead to the practical conclusion that authority can and should be minimized. This is true because the first concept implies the right of individuals to manage their own affairs for better or for worse and because the second implies that we can increasingly place greater reliance upon reason and less upon force. Thus, with the advance of liberal ideas, there was an increasing emphasis upon attaining improvements in human relations through general education, the raising of moral standards, and a quickening of conscience in men's dealings with men. At the same time, there were the efforts to restrict the authority of the state, the power of private groups, and, in general, the authority of man over man. Advances in these lines were among the most striking accomplishments of the eighteenth and nineteenth centuries: the Bill of Rights, abolition of serfdom and slavery, and restrictions on the use of governmental power.

But in the last half century, this trend in Western countries has been reversed. On the part of well-intentioned reformers and the most cynical seekers of individual and group interests alike, there is the same reliance upon force. The chief center of force in the modern world is the state; and, quite generally, proposals for reform have increasingly taken the form of "there ought to be a law" or that some administrative organ of government should be endowed with discretionary power. With some people this reliance upon force frankly goes to the logical extreme of glorifying the omnipotent state; these people are the Socialists and Communists. With others, chief reliance is placed upon functional groups, such as labor unions, farm blocs, or business cartels; but in any event, main reliance upon individual industry, foresight, thrift, or even the altruistic impulses of individuals has declined. The common denominator of this way of thought is that the well-being of individuals is to be entrusted to others who will be empowered to employ pressures (coercion) and, in a wide range of activities, to override the objections of individuals.

This is why it is so difficult for those who today call themselves liberals to distinguish themselves (which they often sincerely desire to do) from the Socialists and Communists. The fact is that, as to the basic issue of the relation of the individual and the group, they are on the same side. The thoroughgoing collectivists would concentrate control in the powerful state; the other economic planners and self-styled liberals of our country would favor a mixture of more comprehensive state control with increasingly powerful occupational groups. With many popular reformers, with moderate Socialists, and with Communists, there is in varying degrees an impatience with the individual who is not in harmony with the generally approved views of the welfare of the group. In a basic sense they are all authoritarian in their approach.

This does not mean that when union leaders, for example, and their spokesmen in politics deny sympathy for communism they are at all insincere. They may indeed be most outspoken enemies of it. But it is a commonly observed fact that the most bitter opposition is often engendered between individuals or groups whose differences are not profound. The great and most bitter religious wars were fought between groups of Christians, whose differences in views were, as we see them today, less marked than their points of agreement. It may even be true at the moment that the best defense against communism is a strong trade union movement, and, on the other hand, it is quite clear that a Communist state would not tolerate trade unions as we know them. But the real antithesis is between those who like and trust power solutions and those who dislike and profoundly distrust them. It is between those who would build up aggregations of power in smaller or larger units and those who would limit or disperse private power groups and limit the use of that residual power which by its nature is entrusted to government.

Majority Rule and its Proper Limits

The traditional liberal philosophy is that individuals cannot be trusted to exercise unchecked power over others. This distrust was especially strong when the directed had no voice in the selection of their directors nor any effective veto upon their orders, but it is not confined to such cases. As Woodrow Wilson once wrote, "The history of liberty has been the history of limitations on the power of the government." The proposition seems equally valid whether the government derives its support from a majority or a minority.

The development of majority rule as a principle of government has, of course, been a great advance in many ways. Some people would assume that it is the most important requirement of a good society. This I think would be an exaggeration.

As we said before, one of the great issues to be decided concerning any society is the relation of man to the group. As long as the group was dominated by small minorities or by dictators it was not difficult to convince reasonable people that the cause of freedom would be advanced by popular election. How our rulers are selected is no doubt an important practical question for good government and especially for determining the organic law by which a people decides on the general type of society under which it wishes to live; but, as to the basic, philosophic, question raised between liberalism and authoritarianism, it is of secondary importance. The more important question is what rights do the 49 percent have against the 51 percent? Or, indeed, what are the rights of one person against the whole nation?

This point seemed to be missed or not accepted by many (probably most) of the leaders of the French Revolution. The hateful thing there was the privilege of the aristocracy which seemed to have no rational justification. This sentiment led to executions, violence, and disorder but it did not provide a sound basis for a government of limited powers.

There has been an important shift of emphasis on these points from the early days of our government to the present. The great liberals of that time were not primarily concerned with majority rule—indeed, perhaps not as much as they should have been—for slavery was indorsed and the suffrage was, of course, quite restricted. But they were vitally concerned with the rights of individuals against *any* government, and they expressed that concern in the principle that the government had only such powers as were expressly granted to it; and, then perhaps superfluously, but just to make doubly sure, they adopted the Bill of Rights.

It is well to remind ourselves and especially the younger generation that the Bill of Rights did not so much *create* rights as to prohibit government from infringing upon those regarded as pre-existent. "The Congress shall make no law respecting an establishment of religion. . . . or abridging freedom of speech," etc. It did not *give* people the right of free speech nor indeed does it protect it except from actions of the government. Indeed in the first instance it applied only to the national government, though this protection has now been largely extended to state governments too.

But the so-called "G.I. Bill of Rights" greatly extended the field of active responsibility of government for the well-being of its citizens. Rights nowadays mean something you can claim, usually from the state. The government is now looked upon as the dispenser of good things and this supports a tendency for growth of government power—especially power of the central government.

Today we are greatly concerned that everyone shall have a voice in selecting his governors, but we are not so much concerned about protecting the individual's rights against those governors. Many people feel that constitutional limitations in the use of power by government should be brushed aside if an act of the legislature is designed for a good purpose and, if the legislation has popular support. Popular leaders who have great power and seek more have ridiculed the notion that free people need to protect themselves from their own government.

This effort of government to woo the people is shown in many ways, for example, by regulatory bodies like the Federal Trade Commission which seeks to create the impression that only its watchful care protects the people. This, of course, implies that the companies against whom they bring cases are, or behave like, enemies of the people. Even in the courts in antitrust cases there is much unctuous talk by the prosecutor to the farmers, tradesmen, and housewives of the jury about "your government." The defense lawyer naturally speaks of *the* government and tries to get the jury to identify themselves with the citizen who is being attacked by these "outlanders" from Washington. It is an amusing epitome of the age-old conflict of man vs. the state, in this case of the citizen vs. the government. But amusing as it may be, a citizen who knows anything of history from the days of the Roman Empire to Hitler, Stalin, and Mussolini can well be excused for instinctively grasping his purse and raising his guard when officials begin to use sweet words about being his servant in the conduct of *his* government. Liberty is better preserved if we think of *the* government. Also this is more accurate. Government is one thing and the people is (or are) another, in spite of the fact that in all countries government must at least be tolerated by a substantial part of the people or that, in our country, it must secure at long intervals the formal approval of an election.

This confusion of thought is reflected in the different uses of the word "we." "We the people" wish to do certain things or "we" as individuals wish to do certain things. These two are by no means the same thing. The writer has tried to make this distinction clear to his students by proposing to them that we decide what we are going to have for lunch and ask how we should proceed. It is usually proposed that we vote on the question. The frequency of this suggestion is a measure of the extent to which the group meaning of we has become established. If this approach is used someone might propose that we have fish; another proposes that we have hash. Now people will begin to take sides and we have a fish party and a hash party. Finally a vote is taken and the hash party wins by one vote. So we all have hash.

Now has this been a great victory for self-government? Well, it is quite possible that hash was not the first choice of any member of the group except probably the person who first proposed it. To the rest of them it might simply have been the less disagreeable choice between fish and hash. Many people feel this way about the results of a national election of a president.

The other meaning of "we" is suggested when some unreconstructed individualist says "to heck with all this voting, let us go to a cafeteria and each person choose what he wants." In this case just as truly as in the other *we* would have decided what *we* want for lunch, but the difference is very great. The decision of the most honest, efficient, and representative government is no substitute for true self-government.

Obviously this is not to say that we never should have common decisions. But, as in the case of the lunch problem, we should ask ourselves seriously: Is there no way in which this problem can be solved by each individual? A group decision backed by government involves coercion. It almost never gains unanimous consent. In a truly free society coercion will be kept to its lowest practical limits. The highest development of statecraft in a free society will be directed to avoiding the necessity of group decisions, because they always involve coercion or the threat of it upon the inevitable minority.

But group decisions do have a great attraction even when they are not truly necessary, for unfortunately, there are certain characteristics of human nature which make it intolerable for many people that some, and particularly a small minority, would be different from others. This seems to be a characteristic of *human* nature; apparently it is also a characteristic of much of animal life. An albino bird will be ostracized by the flock of black birds.

These words are being written the day after a national law was finally passed which assumes that the very complicated and difficult problem of race relations must be solved in the same way in 50 different states—not merely that one basic principle should apply, but that the details, for example, of landlord-tenant and employer-employee relations must be identical. It sometimes seems that how much protection individuals should have against adverse discrimination is not so important as the requirement that the rights of such individuals in one state should be no greater or no less than in another state.

We seem to be approaching rather than moving away from the condition against which John Stuart Mill was warning in 1856 in his *Essay on Liberty*. He said that in the England of his time there seemed to be a growing view that the ideal condition would be for every Englishman to be exactly like every other one.

In some respects the danger of infringement on the freedom of individuals is greater in a democracy than in earlier autocratic forms of government. An unchecked majority certainly can be a worse tyrant than an individual. The individual tyrant, if he is opposed by a large part of the population, will find it very difficult and no doubt indiscreet to try to force his will upon the whole group. Moreover, he may well be deterred either by conscience or at least by a feeling of disapproval of those around him. But the members of a majority support one another in their conviction that their use of power is right and just. All "right thinking people" with whom the members of the majority associate agree.

Another sign of this acceptance of group decisions is in the widespread feeling that the vital question about private groups, as for example labor unions, is whether the officers are honestly selected and responsive to the wishes of the majority. The question whether such representatives of a majority shall have the power to limit the freedom of individuals is pushed into the background. To the traditional liberal the latter is the essential question. Must we not admit that the relative areas of freedom of the individual, on the one side, and of the group's mastery over the individual, on the other, is a more profound question than that of who shall wield the authority for the group? On this question of the individual against the group, traditional liberalism and the modern brand parading under the same name are irreconcilably opposed. There may be, and no doubt there must be, compromises, but the ideals cannot be truly reconciled.

Development of Political Freedom

A number of writers among whom are Mill and Ortega have suggested various stages in the history of political freedom. If one starts with a system of absolutism in Western Europe, we progressed by stages to the present popular government. The first step was the granting of immunities by the ruler to certain individuals or classes of people. This happened in various ways in different countries. On the Continent the developing commercial towns such as Ghent provided a group of people who could and would defy the local feudal lord. This power rested on the fact that these burghers had money, whereas the feudal lords relying more on the self-contained economy of the manor or upon payments in kind had little of that medium and indeed were quite unsophisticated in uses of money. Even the powerful lord was at a disadvantage with the "city slicker." But more and more frequently occasions arose when one of these lords needed money as a dowry for his daughter or to go on a crusade to the Holy Land or some other noneconomic purpose. Then he would go to the traders or bankers. The burghers might well demand certain concessions for the citizens of their town, somewhat like but more useful than, Shylock's demand for the pound of flesh. The feudal lord might well be constrained to grant these concessions. Frequently the canny townsmen insisted that they be written down on parchment. Strong towers can still be seen in certain cities of Europe today where this valued charter or list of immunities was preserved.

The next step was making generalized concessions to certain broad classes of people. Magna Carta was an example, when the king granted a list of very important rights to his lords and barons. Next came the concessions of powers to parliament, which had gained the power to grant or withhold desired revenue from the king. These were sufficiently general to be called constitutional limitations. Next came the power of the people to choose their own governors. At the outset and for a long time thereafter the assertion of the power of the people to select their own governors was not a denial of the distinction between rulers and ruled. What the people had gained was not a power directly to rule themselves, but the power to choose those who would be the rulers. In this stage there was still the fear of excessive government power and much emphasis on constitutional limitations. Under this theory of government, according to Edmund Burke, the voters went to the polls and chose a person in whom they had confidence to make their laws and govern them. In Burke's view it was not the proper function of the voters to specify how their "representative" would vote.

As time went on, however, people did come to take precisely this view. In this country the accession of Andrew Jackson to the Presidency was an important milestone toward this idea. And it has been pretty well accepted today. In this view the ideal, if it were physically possible, would be for all people to vote directly on all legislation. Only because this is impossible, do we elect certain "representatives" who, like spokesmen, are to represent us and vote as we would vote if we were there. Some people regard this as the highest and most desirable development of popular government. Others have regarded it as a retrogression, which if unchecked, would lead back to authoritarianism.

In the strict use of the word, the stage of direct government by an unchecked majority can be called democracy. With the dangers of this kind of government in mind the ancient Greeks regarded democracy as the worst possible form of government. It was a rule by the demos, that is, the mob. With these thoughts in mind the founders of our government talked about a republican form of government or a representative form of government, but not a democracy. The Constitution itself can be regarded as a defense against that form of government. Felix Morley has described the attitudes of the founders.

> The founding fathers certainly had a clear idea of the form of government they were establishing by the Constitution. And the most influential of them were strongly opposed to a democratic political system, meaning one that endeavors to facilitate the triumph of the majority will. In "a pure democracy" wrote Madison, "there is nothing to check the inducements to sacrifice the weaker party or an obnoxious individual. Hence it is that such democracies have ever been spectacles of turbulence and contention; have ever been found incompatible with personal security or the rights of property; and have in general been as short in their lives as they have been violent in their deaths." John Adams, our second President, put it more sharply: "There never was a democracy that did not commit suicide." That was certainly not the system these men were supporting for the United States.
>
> Charles A. Beard, personally one of the most democratic of all our historians, thought it essential to emphasize the undemocratic nature of the American form of government. "At no time," he wrote, "at no place in solemn convention assembled, through no chosen agents, had the American people officially proclaimed the United States to be a democracy. The Constitution did not contain the word or any word lending countenance to it, except possibly the mention of 'we, the people,' in the preamble." [1]

If these fears are well founded it would be quite consistent with many other parts of life in which we find that any principle carried to extreme limits and without checks is less effective than the more moderate position.

The General Will

The case for pure democracy was advanced by the assertion of a "general will," the *volonté générale,* of Jean Jacques Rousseau in the

[1] Morley, *op. cit.,* pp. 12 and 13.

late eighteenth century. The thought was that "the people" in the mass give their approval or disapproval to certain acts or conditions. This then is the "will of the people," which in a democracy was to take the place of "the king wills it." This idea at first sight seems harmless enough. The deeper significance of it was not and is not today apparent to all. If there is a general will which is discernible, then it obviously should be followed if the country pretends to be a government "of the people and for the people." This justifies two propositions, first, that there must be someone or some group who can discern and define this general will and, second, someone or group who will have the power to carry it out. And these two provide the basis for totalitarianism. There must be a priesthood (the interpreters) and an executive. These we find for present-day communism in the high councils of the party. This doctrine also implies that, once the general will has been determined, anyone who dissents from it is an enemy of the people. In modern communism he is called a deviationist; in the history of religion he is a heretic. In the presence of a defined general will neither the deviationist nor the heretic has any rights. The concept of the rights of the individual against the state makes no sense once the idea of a "general will" is accepted.[2]

Rousseau with his concept of the general will had a very great influence on revolutionary sentiment in France and on the course of the French Revolution with its terror and intolerance. The idea provided the ideological backing for Napoleon and his conquests, which were always in the name of the people. This transition from pure democracy to dictatorship was a dramatic demonstration of the dictum of John Adams that a pure democracy would always destroy itself. Somewhat later it became the basis for Marx's "dictatorship of the proletariat" and still later of Hitler and Mussolini's justification for the all encompassing state. Truly few doctrines have better illustrated the words of Auguste Compte that "Ideas rule the world or throw it into chaos."

What effect does this far reaching idea have upon present day democratic societies, including our own? Most Americans would presumably agree that an idea adopted by Congress and approved by the President was at best an expression of a majority and possibly, like our fish-hash example, only a contrived consensus that came closer than anything else to the desires of the whole people or, to express it otherwise, did less violence to the opposed views of the people. It is only a workable compromise. It is doubtful if many would hold that such a specific belief or measure was really the will of the people in some absolute or

[2] On the General Will, see Morley, *op. cit.*, Chapter 3.

mystic sense. But in practice we do come close to acting as though it were.

The general will provided a support for pure democracy so it is not too difficult to reverse the process and deduce the general will from one's desire for a pure democracy. And if one accepts unchecked democracy there is a strong tendency to act as though the mystical concept were real. By 1964, for example, the cause of Negro rights had been so widely accepted by leaders outside the South that anyone who dissented, even on details of legislation, was regarded in cultivated circles as an enemy of the people, or an irresponsible, stupid person whose views obviously did not need to be taken seriously. They could be disregarded as we would disregard the views of children in considering the general will of the country. One didn't argue with a dissenter. Discussion was in terms of "How did the fellow get that way?" as though the holding of a dissenting view on this question was like some mysterious malady.

The founders of our government clearly attempted by limitations on their powers of government and by the separation of the branches of government, to avoid the unbridled power of a majority. If now all departments and branches of government are to act on the basis of (a) what they think is good or (b) on what they believe to be the general will, this system for the protection of rights of individuals will break down and we will be headed for pure democracy. Such a breakdown would occur, for example, if the Supreme Court were to decide questions of constitutionality on the basis of its appraisal of the popular will. So far, at least as an abstract proposition, our people have supported the independence of the Court, as was shown by the reaction to President Roosevelt's effort to dominate it in the interest of his interpretation of the general will. In the recent civil rights cases there have appeared many charges that the Court has merely reflected its own views of desirable public policy or its interpretation of the general will. This writer will not presume to express an opinion on this legal question. He does feel free to point out that it is in just such situations as this, where "justice" and the sentiments of "men of good will" are heavily on one side, that the danger to the defense of liberties, even unpopular ones, is most pronounced. It is in such cases that we could move toward Rousseau's concept of the general will and toward the unfortunate consequences of that philosophy.

The line between pure democracy and pure autocracy is very thin. Once you think of "the people" in mass, not as individuals, and of the will of this mass, the rights of minorities will be neglected and the power of the mass, or of those who claim to speak for it, will be exalted. It is interesting in passing to observe that laws designed to advance the interests of some minorities can be the very instruments for destroying the rights of other minorities. It is well to remember, as we have said before, that the fundamental minority is the minority of one. When the rights of the individual minority are brought down, then the rights of the so-called minority groups have lost their basic support. Then their only protection will be in pandering to or threatening or begging from the majority. This is all one can do against an unchecked "general will."

A more simple way of expressing the similarity of pure democracy and pure autocracy is to note that neither form has any checks. Both are omnipotent. And one recalls the words of Lord Acton: "All power corrupts and absolute power corrupts absolutely."

Limited government is an essential part of the philosophy of a free society basically because limitations are required to leave room for freedom of action for the individual. Superficially the case for unlimited democracy might be appealing, for under it "the people" can theoretically work their will without hindrance. It is only when we recognize that the people collectively is a very different thing from people individually, that the fallacy becomes apparent.

There is, in fact, no "general will" of the people except in the sense of a statistical composite of individual wills, and that is made up of some very diverse wills. That being the case, the good society will keep to the minimum those instances where it finds it necessary to act on this clumsy statistical average instead of allowing people individually to act on their own desires.

Dangers of Groupism

A particular danger of the government attempting to look after the welfare of the people by direct means arises from the fact that the people of the United States constitute almost innumerable groups. There are the occupational groups—the plumbers, the retail druggists, and others; there are the city people and the country people and now a new group, suburbia; there are religious groups; there are much more subtle groupings by intellectual and educational classes, and so on. If now the government is to be used to advance the interest of the "people" it can only do so directly by considering the people in their different groups. Suppose, for example, that it is desired to help the manufacturers of the country or those of a particular line. An obvious way is to protect them from the competition of foreign producers. This the government can easily do by establishing a protective tariff. To succeed in inducing the government to grant this aid those demanding the protection do not have to be a majority of the people; they may be a very small minority. It is sufficient that they be intensely interested at the same time that the many people who perhaps would be disadvantaged by such protection have only a vague and very mild objection. So the special privilege of protection from competition is granted to this group.

Shortly another group, let us say the silver miners, perceive a danger that we may change our coinage system and, thereby, they would be disadvantaged. Hence legislation is proposed requiring the purchase every year of a certain amount of silver. Again the active and very vocal minority may well prevail. What does the average voter know or care about the government buying silver for coins? Thus we could go on through various groups of people; farmers, retail druggists, factory workers, farm workers to school teachers and professional workers, each one asking for its own special class of legislation. Suppose as we go along this road some statesman recognizes that virtually every one of these special bits of legislation is designed to benefit one group at the expense of the whole society. More specifically, suppose he finds that most of them involve a restriction of output of the particular category concerned, which raises the price of this particular product or service at the expense of the rest of the society. He might point out that it is an error to conclude that because a certain kind of policy is good for A and good for B and good for C it must, therefore, be good for the community of ABC. This does not follow. It is the "error of composition." Restriction of output by A may benefit A. Restriction of output by B may benefit B and so for C, but the restriction of output by ABC together leads to reduced output all around and, followed far enough, to economic suicide for the whole community.

Our clearsighted statesman might now say that it is obvious that we are on the wrong track. We should reverse our course and remove those special privileges already given to A, B, and C, because if we keep them X, Y, and Z and others are going to demand the same sort of special treatment. If our statesman did seriously entertain this idea it would surely show that, statesman though he was, he was no politician. Very soon he or his successor would observe that it is much easier to remove comparative inequities between the favored groups and the others by granting equal privileges to X, Y, and Z rather than taking them away from A, B, and C.

If we follow this politically realistic line of reasoning the democracy can get farther and farther into the welter of special privileges till we have what Walter Lippmann once called a system of special privileges for all. This is quite obviously a contradiction in terms, because the very nature of a privilege is that it must be special. If such a system goes far enough, as it had, for example, it Italy after World War I, the demand for some strong man or men who will be immune to the pressures of the groups could very well become the most promising way out of the dilemma.

The conclusion from these observations is that the general welfare which is to be sought in a free society should have only a very general meaning. It can properly refer to the establishment of a social and economic environment which will be favorable to the pursuit of happiness. When we attempt to carry the idea further than this we get into an unseemly scramble for advantages by hundreds of groups and thousands of individuals which becomes a "beggar-my-neighbor" mess.

Since this is fundamentally an ineffective organization of society, it must ultimately break down, either from internal forces or from pressures from the outside. We can well recall that Arnold Toynbee in his *Study of History* identifies 21 different civilizations that have existed in the history of the world. Some of them have disappeared completely. Some are in an arrested state. Some are definitely on the decline and he thinks only one, namely, our Western civilization based on Roman and Greek antecedents is still vital.

Viewing the ways in which societies and forms of government have evolved, it would be well for us to consider carefully whether unlimited government dedicated directly to advancing the welfare of the people does indeed represent the highest stage of social organization, or whether it represents a passing of the apex and the beginning of the decline. We cannot prove with historical evidence that individual freedom and the development of individuality gives the best assurance of progress and survival, though John Stuart Mill makes a good case for the theory that the reason for Western Europe's greater advance in the past 2,000 years than China's, was its greater variety of conditions human and natural. And he argues persuasively that this progress will cease when the variety disappears. An all-powerful government, regardless of its claims to legitimacy, is an enemy of variety, individual differences and hence of creativity. If these considerations of the value of variety for national preservation have any merit, and even more if we accept freedom and variety for their own sake, we should give careful thought to the requirements that a society aiming at these ends imposes. One of these is that we should not rely too heavily on the government to provide the good society.

Economic Freedom

An implication of the exaltation of the individual is that he shall have the maximum of freedom of choice in all his activities. In the religious sphere, this means that he shall be free to choose his own religion; in the civil field that he shall be free to hold and express opinions of his own; and in the political field that he shall be free to exercise his vote to choose his own governors. But there is also the essential matter of freedom in the economic field which we cannot separate from the other freedoms.

In the first place, freedom in the economic field means that consumers shall be free to buy or to save. They must be free to exercise such purchasing power as they have to buy what they please. This proposition rules out sumptuary laws and regulations, which were very common in the past and which attempted to direct the consumption of the people in such a way as to advance the welfare of the state or of the people themselves.

The freedom of people as consumers must also extend to a choice of where and from whom they shall buy. It is thus the basis of free trade, both within the country and between countries. Within the country consumers must be free to choose between alternative sellers, and this means that there *must be* alternative sellers. The author of the famous Beveridge plan in England, for all his protestations about the importance of "essential" freedoms, did not appear to recognize this point, for he asserts that the freedom to establish or operate a business is not an essential one. But if individuals can only buy from those limited sources to whom the state has given a license to engage as enterprisers and sellers or, still worse, if they can only buy from the state itself, surely their own freedom of choice has been limited. This instance illustrates, as well as any, the difficulty of limiting freedom in some areas and of some important groups without limiting the freedom of all others.

Economic freedom should also include the freedom of individuals as workers to determine for themselves how much they shall work, how hard they shall work, in what lines of activity they shall work, and in what parts of the country they shall work. The highest practical degree of freedom in this respect, as in all the others, will fall short of perfection, for it is clear that some individuals will be precluded from engaging in certain occupations because of physical handicaps, intellectual limitations, and lack of training. This freedom is also limited at times by the general level of employment. It is, nevertheless, an ideal toward which we should strive.

While these conditions cannot be guaranteed, the state at least can avoid on its own behalf the imposition of barriers. Further, it can and should use its influence to prevent private groups from imposing such barriers—for example, the limitations placed upon freedom of entry by certain labor unions and the limitations placed by many of the states upon the migration of professional workers. Still further, the state can enhance this freedom of choice by an effective employment service, by the dissemination of information about job opportunities, and by job training programs. Indeed, the whole field of education has the effect of enhancing freedom of choice in employment.

The freedom of workers, as part of the concept of economic freedom, encounters serious obstacles in any society which attempts extensive economic planning. For in such a society there must be certain objectives as to the kinds of goods and the relative quantities of goods to be produced. Under such a system the workers of the country must be regarded as "manpower." We all use this term at times as a form of verbal shorthand to mean the whole lot of individual workers, but it is sometimes used with an implication that is obnoxious to thoughtful liberals. For to them one cannot talk about human beings as though they were bricks or *things*. Even in the short period after the war in which the ideals of the planned economy prevailed in England, there was a disconcerting tendency on the part of the state to deal with workers as *things*. For example, under the regulations any unemployed person must seek employment through the national employment service, and he must be willing to accept employment in those places and occupations to which he may be directed on pain of denial of unemployment benefits if he refuses to conform.

Economic freedom should also extend to enterprisers. Individuals should ideally have the choice of being hired men or self-employed or of employing others. A society, to realize these ideals, must have a considerable flexibility and variety in its economic organization. Large business organizations must occupy part of the field in the interest of efficiency and cost reduction as well as to provide opportunities for the thousands of people who would prefer to be employed rather than to assume the risks and responsibilities of being employers. But a good society must also maintain a favorable environment for small business, for those who prefer the way of life which that type of enterprise provides both for employers and employees. And this environment should also be one that is favorable to small businesses becoming large businesses, for that is one of the natural ambitions of small enterprisers.

Finally, the ideal of freedom of choice will, under a liberal philosophy, be extended to other societies. Under it, no one national sovereignty, nor even any prospective world sovereignty, should presume to limit the freedom of choice of another country as long as that country does not interfere with the freedom of others.

This suggests a general observation on all of these forms of economic freedom, namely, that the freedom of one unit must be limited when its exercise infringes seriously upon the similar freedom of others. It is admittedly difficult to draw this line. It is clear that the freedom of individuals to use narcotics can properly be restricted because of the harm that addicts may do to others. It is likewise clear that in certain lines workers should not be permitted to practice an art or profession unless they are adequately prepared, because again they may do positive harm to others. Enterprisers also may properly be restricted from producing and selling goods which are positively harmful. Lastly, one country or a combination of them may properly bring pressures to bear upon practices of a foreign country that interfere with the freedom of others. But even under a broad interpretation of this principle, we are rarely justified in requiring individuals to act positively in such ways as the authority may believe would contribute most to the general welfare. For that welfare includes freedom as one of its most important elements.

Equality of Opportunity

What we have said about extension of the area of freedom of choice implies a maximizing of opportunities. In a free society, opportunities for individuals to realize their greatest potentialities should be maintained with as little interference as possible. Now we need to add that, under the liberal concept of the good society, this opportunity should be, as nearly as possible, equal for all citizens. Equality of opportunity can best be understood by contrast to its opposite, which is privilege. The meaning of "privilege" in its strict sense is suggested by its etymological origin, a combination of the terms *privus* and *lex,* that is, private law. Privilege thus derives from those special concessions and rights granted in the pre-liberal age by the sovereign to certain individuals or groups of individuals as a peculiar benefit to be enjoyed by them alone. It, therefore, implied a derogation of the rights of others. So the word in its proper meaning implies an advantage over others. It is thus the opposite of equal rights and equal opportunities.

In the philosophy of a free society these privileges should be reduced to the minimum. In the words of Abraham Lincoln, it is the duty of government toward men "to lift all artificial weights from their shoulders, to clear the paths of laudable pursuits for all; to afford all an unfettered start in the race of life." That brief statement can stand as an expression of one of the important aspects of the philosophy of liberalism.

There are some who attach little importance to this requirement. One very erudite European social philosopher for whom the writer has high respect regards inequality of opportunity as largely created by the achievements of one's parents, which give superior educational opportunities as well as inheritance of wealth. To him the freedom of the man of one generation to provide well for his children is essential to a free society. It tends to maintain a family continuity and to him the family is perhaps even more important than the individual. There is some validity in this contention, and in any event surely it is true that, after everything possible has been done to provide equality of opportunity, important unavoidable differences will exist. For example, the inheritance of intellectual qualities and the influence of growing up in a cultured family can never be abolished. But as Lincoln's statement implies we should remove "artificial" weights and clear the paths of laudable pursuits.

It is important that we do this if we are to justify unequal rewards. People generally will accept without too much bitterness the superior position and supply of goods of another if he can see a plausibly reasonable explanation for it; if, for example, he can believe that "we all had an even start. Perhaps the other chaps performed better or got the breaks, but at any rate the social system did not stack the cards against me." A good society must be one in which there is some apparently acceptable basis on which rewards are provided. From the point of view of a stable society this is perhaps the most important requirement of all.

So it seems that a good society will do what can be done (1) to provide equal opportunity and (2) unequal rewards. It works both ways, for there is no sense in worrying about having the racers start precisely even in the race of life if they are going to get the same reward anyway. The equal opportunities justify the unequal rewards, and the unequal rewards give justification for efforts to provide equal opportunities.

One of the most important privileges that people in many countries have in modern times is education. Accordingly, it has been quite consistent with the liberal view to extend the opportunities of education to ever wider groups of citizens and to ever rising levels.

Historically, the other great source of privilege has been inheritance of property. We do place limits upon inherited wealth or position as part of an effort to give equal opportunities. But most of the impetus for highly progressive estate taxes and inheritance taxes comes, I fear, from a plain desire for equality of condition, not merely of opportunity.

There are two reasons for giving less attention to inheritance than to the education. One of these is that use of inheritance taxes for this purpose has the disadvantage that in striving for equality of opportunity of the younger generation the state is infringing upon the freedom of the older generation to accumulate and use the accumulation for the benefit of its family. The other is that inequality of this kind is much less important than that of education. Especially in these later days opportunities to advance to the highest positions in industry do not require inherited wealth. They do depend very heavily upon natural abilities and education. Also marrying the boss' daughter helps, but ability and education play their part even in that.

Federalism

For preserving a free society, especially in a large country, the most favorable form of government is a federal system, i.e., federalism. This has been the form of government of the United States from the beginning. It means that authority and power is divided between several governmental units, specifically between the central government and the governments of the several states. We may well pause here to recognize another popular misuse of terms comparable to that of "liberal." The government at Washington is often and even in official usage described as the Federal Government. The mere existence of a strong government in Washington would not in itself imply a federal system. Indeed if nothing else were considered it would imply the opposite, a highly centralized government like that of France, in which the government of all parts proceeds from Paris. Certainly this has not been the accepted theory in the United States, where the states have their own areas of sovereignty and the central government has its. The term Federal Government should logically refer to a complex of 51 centers of government —50 state governments and one central government.

How did we slip into the usage? Perhaps because at the outset after the sovereignty of the Crown had been repudiated and before our Constitution was established the states were indeed sovereign—completely so. The forming of the union was only accomplished by the states yielding some of this sovereignty to a new unit, the central government. Thus in a very real sense the central government was formed by the states. This is true in spite of the mellifluous phrase in the preamble, "we the people," a phrase which was opposed by Patrick Henry and others who felt it should be "we the several states." At any rate it was generally reorganized that the government at Washington owed its existence to the federation and hence was called the Federal Government. Of course, we cannot change our language, but it may be well for thoughtful people to recognize that the dichotomy is between "central" or "national" government or "general" government on the one hand and "state" or "local" government on the other. The balanced system comprising the two is the Federal[3] Government and the abstract principle of this balanced system is "federalism."

Now what is the relation of the philosophy of a free society to this principle of federalism? The relation shows itself in several ways. One of these is that a free society in our American conception rejects, and we think must reject, pure democracy as its governmental form. The reason for this is that pure democracy means the unchecked power of a majority, which leaves no place for the rights of minorities. If we are to have, therefore, a government which in its very form protects the rights of minorities, limitations on the powers of the government must be established and preserved in the organic law. There are several ways in which this can be done. One of them, of course, is the adoption of a written constitution which grants specified powers to government—in our case to the national government. Any powers not so granted are denied to it and are reserved to the states and to the people. By this device it was supposed that the power of the central government was definitely restricted and, of course, the powers of the state government were also restricted by the grants which they had made to the national government. By this process minority rights of a certain kind were to be protected. This particular kind was the minority represented by a geographic area.

There are various other ways in which the power of the government is restricted from what it would be in a pure democracy. Among these are limitations imposed on the national government by the Bill of Rights. The powers of the state governments are also limited by the Bill of Rights which most of them have adopted and also by certain judicial interpretations which have extended the limitations upon the national government in the Bill of Rights to the several states. Thus the significance of the original Bill of Rights, which limited the powers only of the national government, has gradually been so extended that it covers

[3] Another mischievous effect of this confusion is that many people regard a growth of the power of the "federal" (central) government as an extension of federalism, whereas it is more reasonable to say that such an extension threatens to destroy federalism.

all forms of government. We can say "all forms" because the local government, cities, villages, counties, and so on, are creatures of the states and, therefore, their only powers are those granted by the states. Thus in an important sense we can say the states are the basic units for the powers of the central government were granted by the states in the first place and the smaller units are literally creatures of the states.

Another way in which we avoid the evils of pure democracy is in the checks and balances existing between the branches of government—the power of veto held by the executive over the legislature and the independent judiciary which is not supposed to be responsive to the will of the people. So we cannot say that the federal system is the only check upon unlimited powers of the national government, but it is, nevertheless, one of the important ones.

It is one which seems especially important in a large country. It is very doubtful if a free society could be maintained in a country as large as ours or Russia's, for example, in the absence of the federal principle. A reason for this view is that if one tries to legislate on local problems from one central place thousands of miles away he must inevitably, and even with the best intentions, impose legislation upon the whole country which will be quite offensive to certain parts of it.

The federal principle recognizes that in some areas of legislation this overriding of the local desires may be inevitable. For example, we must declare war or conclude a peace on the basis of the whole nation, even though certain sections may disagree. But on the other hand, in the great area of ordinary affairs of life such as property laws, marriage, divorce, traffic laws, and so on, and also as to voting requirements, except for the amendments to the Constitution prohibiting discrimination on the basis of race or sex, the federal philosophy holds that there is no objection to diversity, or if some objection does exist that it is much overweighed by the advantages of local approval for legislation in these fields. In short, in the absence of a federal system one must, as a practical matter, impose uniformity upon areas in which the conditions and attitudes of the people are quite different.

We say one *must* impose this uniformity. Actually attempts have been made in some centralized governments to legislate differently for the different communities. For example, Colbert, the great finance minister under Louis XIV, attempted to specify the particular kinds of cloth that could be made in each of the different communities of France. His regulations went so far as to specify the number of threads per inch that must be used in the cloth in the city of Dijon and other numbers for the various other communities. Actually, although the orders were issued from Paris, one might argue that this was a form of local government, though of an objectionable kind, because quite obviously the ministry in Paris knew little about the textile industry of each community. What they did was to accept the recommendations of the established manufacturers in these communities, and the system therefore became one of protection of existing producers against newcomers who might like to do business in some other way. The central government actually was only placing its stamp of approval upon the decisions of certain power groups in the localities.

But generally speaking, it is quite clear that if the legislation on most matters is to proceed from Washington it must be a uniform legislation for all of the country. And if it is uniform, then almost certainly it is going to ride roughshod over the desires of substantial parts of the country. To that extent, the freedom of people in those areas is impaired. Majority rule as remarked before is a poor substitute for individual rule. But, even so, the decision of a majority of the people in a particular community does less violence to individual desires than does a decision by a majority of all of the people of the United States in passing a rule to be imposed upon that community.

This suggests a fundamental basis for federalism. It proceeds from our concept of the importance of the individual. The supposed importance of the individual implies that he should be allowed to do as he pleases just as far as possible, recognizing, of course, that the interdependent society makes some limitations necessary. The closer the setting of these limitations are to the "grass roots," the less the likelihood of serious restrictions upon the will of the individual.

The point can be suggested in a formalistic illustration. Suppose we start with an individual A who is living a Robinson Crusoe existence. As far as limitations placed upon his freedom by others, he is absolutely free. Suppose now that another individual appears and the two recognize the advantages of working together. Once such a partnership has been formed A will not have complete liberty, nor will B. We might conceive that A has given up 50 percent of his freedom on those matters which they need to decide jointly. But we would all recognize that when A is one of a two-man partnership he still has considerable individual influence. Suppose now that the partnership is increased to include 100 men. Then it is quite clear that the individual influence of A in conducting the affairs of the partnership has been considerably reduced. Indeed it is reduced to about one one-hundredth. If now we think of the partnership as consisting of 190 million people then his freedom on any matter which is to be decided jointly is reduced to an infinitesimal amount.

The second point to be deduced from this illustration is that if his condition as to geographic location, social classes, climatic conditions, and others are quite different from those of the great majority, then the infringements upon what he would like to do will be still greater. These limitations can be minimized in the first place by keeping the size of the group which is going to make the joint decisions as small as is feasible, and in the second place, by including in the groups as nearly as possible people of homogeneous attitudes, desires, and conditions. These ideals are approached under federalism.

A basic characteristic of federalism then is that it recognizes and values diversity. It rejects the idea that there is one best way of dealing with the problems of mankind. It is therefore a pluralistic system which is more favorable to individual freedom than is a monolithic system.

Aside from these basic considerations there are certain very practical advantages in a federal system. Such a system is decentralized. The advantages of decentralization are applicable not only to government but to industrial affairs. One of the greatest advances in management technique and in the principles of organization in the last half century in the United States has been the adoption and extension of the principle of decentralized control of some activities, combined with centralization of other activities. The outstanding example, because of the size of the organization (the world's largest industrial concern), because of its admittedly great success, and because of the leadership which is management in decades past provided in the development of this type of organization is the General Motors Corporation. Some people refer to this as a decentralized system, emphasizing thereby the power and autonomy of the several divisions. Others would call it a centralized system emphasizing the ultimate power of central management. Actually it is a mixture of both, a point which has recently been emphasized by Mr. Sloan in his book describing the development of the corporation.[4] It has required a considerable amount of business genius to hit upon and to maintain the most desirable balance between the decisions of the top management and of the divisions such as Chevrolet, Pontiac, and others. This highly efficient organization is really a splendid example of the advantages of federalism.

Under this system in the General Motors Corporation as well as in government there is the opportunity for freedom of experimentation on

[4] Alfred P. Sloan, Jr., *My Years with General Motors* (New York, 1963).

the part of the different units and the opportunity for one division to demonstrate to the others that its way has certain advantages which the others are free to observe and to adopt if they feel it would be helpful. In some of the larger questions such as the relation of one name of car to others in the line the central administration must make the decision. This is comparable to the relationship existing between the states and to the power that is given to the national government under the interstate commerce clause of the Constitution.

A consideration applicable to industrial corporations and government alike is the greater attention which will be given to economical administration in small governmental units than in large ones. An example that came under my personal attention might be offered. It arose at a time when the writer was a member of the Ann Arbor City Council. The chief of the fire department came to the Council and asked for an appropriation for a substantial amount of new fire hose. The reaction of the Council to this was very much the same as would be the reaction of the head of a family to a proposal concerning a family need. The chief was asked whether the old hose was entirely past redemption, whether it would be possible to patch some of it and, therefore, to buy only half the amount which he was proposing. On these points he was not very positive, so a committee was appointed by the Council actually to look at the hose and determine how much of it could be salvaged. They made an on-the-spot investigation and came back with a recommendation for an appropriation approximately two-thirds of what was originally requested. To one accustomed to observing the appropriation procedures in the national government it was in a way an amusing sight to see the members of the City Council personally going to the fire house and making an actual inspection of the fire hose with a view to saving a few thousand dollars. But in another sense it was not ridiculous at all. Here was responsible government at its very best, because the councilmen were saying that, of course, we want to buy this hose if it is actually needed, but we do not want to waste money. It was their own money and that of their immediate neighbors.

Another incident involved the approval of a public improvement which would serve ten houses in a new area. Actually the cost was very high in proportion to the number of houses. I protested that it did not make very good sense to spend $10,000 per house for this purpose when the houses themselves would probably not be worth over $15,000 each. Then the older hands on the council patiently explained to me that 90 percent of the money would come from Washington. All we needed to consider was the remaining 10 percent. That we were also taxpayers to the national government did not register as very important, and as a practical matter it wasn't. This particular project would have an indefinite and very small effect on our own taxes. If our city did not accept the money some other city would accept it. These are the usual arguments, and they are quite logical. But they do add up to irresponsible government, by which I mean that steps are taken without a due regard to the relation between the value of what is to be obtained and the cost thereof. This is not an argument for penny pinching. I was very proud of the people of my city when the property holders voted a very substantial amount for a new high school, knowing full well that they and only they were going to pay for it. This too is responsible government.

The state government has a number of reasons for being more economical and responsible in the spending of money than has the national government. One is the point just mentioned that it is closer to the voters and taxpayers. Another is that the State of Michigan has no possible way of paying for anything except through taxes or borrowing that must be repaid by the State of Michigan. And borrowing is limited by the attractiveness of the bonds, just as it would be for a private corporation. Such limits do not apply to the national government. For the Constitution gives to the national government the power to regulate the currency. This means to print money if necessary. A national government, therefore, is the only entity that readily comes to mind which can adjust its income to its outgo. The rest of us must adjust our outgo to our income, and this goes for all of the governmental units in the country except the national government.

There seems to be no doubt that we have retreated from the principle of federalism in the direction of ever-increasing power of the central government. This is a process which seems to have gone on through most of the history of the country and to have been accelerated in the last few years. As this is being written the President has referred scornfully to those who would look upon this country as merely a federation of 50 separate nations. Of course, they are not separate nations, but neither are they mere historical accidents or arbitrarily constituted administrative units of one great government. Some of the talk on this subject would lead us to expect that the area of legislation of our state legislatures will become progressively smaller and who knows but that our governors may one day be appointed from Washington? Strange views to be conjured up by the remarks of a citizen of the Sovereign

State of Texas, where a favorite quip used to be that the greatest mistake Texas ever made was when it took the rest of the country into the Union.

The tendency to expand the power of the central government seems to have persisted throughout most of the history of the country. Perhaps the basic reason is that at the outset we were dealing with sovereign states which were loath to grant adequate powers to the national government. But any government unit, such as the national government, has a natural inclination to increase its power. There were probably some sound reasons why this should be done. Among these was the great increase in interstate commerce and increased importance of the public lands and of national defense. Then in addition to these legitimate and natural reasons, there is the simple fact that a national government can marshal very considerable power because it can draw upon the resources of all of the states for overcoming the objections of any one of them. A power so possessed will probably be used. This can be very effectively done if the Supreme Court or the other courts of the national government approve and if one can deal with the individual states separately. In the case of the Civil War a considerable part of the country joined together to resist this extension of the central government power. In such a case the outcome can be settled only by resort to war. But in most cases the dissenters will be individual states and they will be unable to combine in effective resistance. Moreover, as was mentioned before, the central government has or can always get the money.

A characteristic of the American people is also relevant. It is the greater interest in substantive problems than in questions of the theory of government. For example, there is a widespread desire recently for greater support for education, particularly for higher education. The state legislatures, working under the requirement that for every million dollars they appropriate they must raise a million dollars in taxes, naturally resist some of the very large demands for education, although on the whole they have been liberal. When this resistance is met there is a natural tendency to turn to Washington. This is met by an almost equal enthusiasm to assist the states on the part of "Washington," meaning by that term the heads of various bureaus which would be involved in the administration of the funds.

Of course, if one asked the question where is the central government going to get the money, obviously the answer is they must get it from the same people as are citizens of the several states. They may get it by the process of inflation rather than by honest and straightforward taxation, but this is only another way of extracting values from the people. The burden has to be borne by the people in either event. This fact has been pointed out over and over again, usually with the additional point that when the dollars go to Washington and come back to your state some of it is going to stick on the hands of the people in Washington. But all these preachments seem to have relatively little effect. There is always the hope that the hundred million dollars to be spent in our state will not be precisely matched by a hundred million dollars of tax burden upon the people of our state. Of course, in total this is a vain hope.

Then when a plan of national aid to the states is set up, every state wants to get some of the aid. On a number of questions such as education many generous people might agree that a system should be set up whereby the more affluent states will contribute to the support of education in the less affluent states. This would be a process of equalizing which, in view of the problems caused by illiteracy, might well be justified if not carried too far. The fact, however, is that when these proposals are made the State of New York, the State of California, and the other affluent states also wish to receive aid from the national government on the theory that if one state is going to get aid then the others should too. Thus this modicum of reason for the whole country assuming some of these local burdens vanishes.

A somewhat related problem, although it does not necessarily involve the expenditure of money, is the desire of people of certain parts of the country representing a majority of the population to impose their will on the whole country thereby running positively counter to the desires of some other important sections. If, for example, the lot of the Negro needs and deserves to be improved and a high degree of emotionalism is aroused by the contest and if it is seen that legislation can be passed on this subject for the whole country, there are very few indeed who will stop to consider the dangers that are involved in an extension of the power of the national government. We should (but do not) consider that the pet project which we would like to get through now and which can be forced upon some dissident states by the power of the central government may some day be balanced by some project which the rest of the United States wants and our state does not want. In this contest of ideas the appeal of the universal settlement is very great. The fact seems to be that we do not like people to be different.

It is a commonly observed fact that Americans contribute more heavily and not merely in proportion to their income but larger parts of their incomes for general public causes, such as support of the Red Cross, the endowment and support of local hospitals, and so on, than do the people of, let us say, England or almost any other country where the policies of the so-called welfare state have been further advanced. There may be a tangible reason for this in that if the government takes so much from the citizen in taxes he will not have enough left for private contribution, but it seems also to be a matter of the shifting of responsibility. Once the idea is established that the state ought to look after any particular need there is a very natural tendency for the citizen to drop his own interest in it.

The projects of local governments dealing with one's own community frequently do arouse more personal interest of the people than those of the national government. Citizens work on committees or serve on government bodies without compensation and really become involved in common projects if these are not too large or too far away. For example, in my home town a sum of over a million dollars recently was given to the city for the care of our trees by a lady who had been a lifelong resident.

The number of problems that have to be solved on a national basis is, of course, increasing, but this fact should not be taken as an excuse to go farther than necessary. There is a tendency to do this and it should be resisted if we desire to keep a sound government for a free society.

There is much that is fine about local government. The government of the small community as recognized by the Ancient Greeks calls forth responsible citizenship. It is likely to be economical; it expresses the consensus of the community and while there will, of course, be dissenting minorities on most questions, these minorities will be a smaller proportion of the people than is the case where the majority consists of people from other parts of the country and the "minority" in the national scene is actually a majority in the locality. These are some of the considerations which establish a close relation between the philosophy of a free society, that is to say, of a good society and the principle of federalism.

XII.

SOME COROLLARIES

The philosophy of a free society regards the free working of natural forces as, on the whole, beneficent. This is not to identify it with a naive view that "God's in His heaven and all's right with the world," nor that this is the best of all possible worlds, nor in any other respect a "Pollyanna" attitude. But neither is it an attitude that life is essentially mean and that one man's hand is naturally against another's as Thomas Hobbes once wrote. Nor is it naturally a world of conflict as Marx pictured it when he said that the history of the world to the present time has been a history of class conflict. The wide diffusion of the views of Marx, though their origin is not always recognized, helps to explain the increasing practice of referring to every program of improvement as a "struggle" for this or a "battle" against this or a "war against poverty" or what would you, always with the implication that it is only the leader and his happy little band of followers who are the people of good will and that arrayed against them are the great forces of ill will and evil.

A young writer in our college paper recently observed that every step forward made by mankind has been the result of a struggle and a fight. This is plain nonsense. The major things that have led to the high standard of living in the United States and to many other good things which we enjoy have come about as a natural result of the development of industry and science and of the activities of hundreds of thousands of enterprising men. They were results which required effort, it is true, and we should not take progress for granted. But they are not in the nature of a conflict against some evil group of people who would like to restrain them. The philosophy of a free society, in other words, is a healthy view which does not indulge in devil seeking or unnecessarily aligning people into hostile camps. It is on the whole an optimistic philosophy.

From this general view flow certain corollaries. We shall mention and comment upon five of them. One is that the interests of economic groups are essentially harmonious. Another is that the effect of competive capitalism is to reduce inequalities. A third is that the increasing affluence of our society provides an opportunity for people individually to gain greater freedoms of choice than ever before. Another is that freedom of trade between parts of the country and between different countries and between individuals in these countries is economically good. And lastly, that a free system within a country and in trade between countries creates a natural force for peace.

Mutual Interests of Economic Groups

There is a widespread and very simple view that in this world what one person gains another one loses. This simple and unattractive view is basic to the philosophy of communism. Bertrand Russell, himself for a long time quite favorable to socialism, remarked that Marx only pretended that he loved the proletariat; actually he only hated the capitalist. It seems a generally justified statement that communism rests upon hatred. It must have its enemies. The workers had to overthrow the capitalists to start with. Then they have to be continually on guard that the capitalists will not "enslave them" again. Then they must guard against and fight the deviationists in their own camp, and so on.

The philosophy and theory of a free enterprise society, on the contrary, asserts that the interests of labor, capital, management, and consumers are basically harmonious. This belief does not rest on a presumed prevalence of brotherly love, but mainly on enlightened self-interest. A basic epigram was given to me as a college youth by an eminent scholar of that time which has literally become the central proposition of my own study of economics. It was that "the value of any one factor of production depends upon the supply of the other factors of production." Upon examination this apparently dry-as-dust proposition is shot through with significance. It provides a basis not only for analysis of economic problems but for a whole outlook on life. For what it says is that the most important requirement for a high value of workers' services is that there should be a large supply of resources and a large supply of capital and a large supply of enterprisers. Under these conditions the value of labor will be high. If a labor leader is truly interested in the welfare of his followers, and if he were a praying man, it would be quite appropriate for him to pray every night for an increased number and prosperity of the capitalists. Likewise, the owners of land can well hope for an increase in population, an increase in the amount of capital, an increase in the amount of labor, and an increase in the amount of management. In any policies, governmental or otherwise, that he recommends he should be solicitous for the welfare and increase of these "other" factors.

The principle holds over an extremely wide range. It can be applied to a particular individual who is head of one of the world's largest corporations. He receives a very large income. He is deluding himself if he thinks this is mainly due to his own abilities. While he receives hundreds of thousands of dollars as head of a great industrial empire, he with the same abilities could obviously not receive anything like that amount if he were head of a small manufacturing concern. The size of the concern, that is the large supply of all the "other" factors, makes his services valuable. The value of everything and all kinds of services depends upon the other things and services which must be used in combination. A certain high grade of administrative ability can have very high value in an environment of large organizations, plentiful supply of labor, adequate supply of capital. It could be almost worthless where these other factors of the economic "mix" were absent.

The failure to see this basic truth underlies some confused thinking on the part of businessmen and others. They often remark that the increased wages of labor have no doubt come from increased productivity of labor. However, it was not the workers who created the increased productivity but the managers, the inventors, and the capitalists. In a very literal sense this is true, but to conclude from this that the advance in the value of labor and its wages is unnatural is a gross error.

The way of economic nature: it is to reward the scarce factor in any necessary combination; and a factor becomes scarce by having a large supply of the others that would normally go with it.

If one wants to put this in more technical terms he can say that the marginal productivity of labor is high when it is placed in combination with a plentiful supply of the other factors which necessarily accompany it. A corresponding statement can be made for the marginal productivity of capital, for the marginal productivity of land, or for the marginal productivity of management. And the value of any one of these factors depends upon its marginal productivity.

According to this view the explanation of the tremendous advance in the national level of real wages in the United States in recent decades does not come from the artificially created bargaining position of labor created by joining unions. This erroneous view comes from confusing the undoubted gains made by some workers, such as stagehands, bricklayers and others with the national average or level of real wages. Union gains in wages are largely acquisitive in the sense that the gains of one group are at the expense of others—and these others are not primarily capitalists and landlords, but other workers. The nature and source of the gains made by some unions will be clarified if one could imagine one big union which included everyone who gains his income from work, i.e., services of some kind. It would thus include everyone except a few idle coupon clippers, who live on pure property income or subsidies. Suppose now that you were elected head of this union and in your acceptance speech you feel obligated to recommend a national policy to improve the lot of your members. You can't very well recommend a demand for higher wages backed by a threat of strike, for your members would be paying the wages as well as receiving them. The only sound advice is to work harder and more effectively in an effort to increase the national income and you don't need a union for that. It is quite probable that the list of dues-paying members would decline. If it declined far enough, it might again become effective, for those in the union could perhaps gain something from those not in.

A union may well be valuable to its members. But it is very doubtful if unions as a whole have increased the income of workers as a whole. The great gains in income of labor come from the fact that labor in this country is scarce relative to the other factors of production and is therefore valuable. Every country has some factor which is its scarce factor. From the point of view of labor and probably from the point of human welfare in general, the United States is fortunate that labor is its scarce factor. After all, we are all people—not acres of land or blocks of capital.

This is not to pass judgment on some good things and certainly some very bad things that have been brought about by the labor unions. It is to assert that a superior standard of living for any country depends upon and will always depend upon much more basic, universal, and permanent factors than the way in which workers are or are not organized.

A summary statement then of this view is that it is not primarily conflict and fight which improves the position of particular classes, but the natural working of sound and impersonal economic forces. It is the beneficent fact that the output, and hence the value, of anyone engaged in production is advanced by the prosperity and healthy growth of the others, whose services or resources are required for the end product. It is a philosophy that all of us in society, if we conduct our affairs sensibly, will be supporting one another. It is the opposite of a philosophy of "beggar my neighbor." It illustrates the words of St. Paul, "ye are all members of one body" or in less elegant modern terms, "we are all in the same boat."

In emphasizing the prevalence of this principle of mutuality of interests of economic groups, we must note another relation not so much between economic groups as between individuals. This is the principle of competition. Workers benefit from an increased supply of capital. They may not benefit by an increased supply of workers, especially of their own kind. Likewise a retail grocer may not benefit from an increase in the supply of retail grocers. The relation of one worker to others who would invade his field, or of one retailer to another of his same kind, is a competitive rather than a complementing relation.

This competitive rivalry between members of one economic group provides a necessary discipline and a directive force in the society. But we should recognize who are rivals and who are complementary. Retailers and customers are not rivals. It is true that the customer may in a short-run view want low prices and the retailer high prices. But the true relationship is revealed if we ask, would a retailer be benefited by having more retailers or more customers? Obviously the latter. Will carpenters be more benefited by having more carpenters in the community or more house builders? Obviously the latter. There is more economic justification for carpenters loving the house builders than other carpenters. The sentiment of solidarity which workers extend to other workers and of opposition and sometimes hatred of the employer must be based upon psychological affinity for "birds of a feather" rather than the logic of an economic man.

There is plenty of room and need for rivalry in a good society. This is a reason why we have laws against restraint of trade, which is another term for restricting competition. This kind of opposition is good. The strengthening of functional groups—e.g., farmers, industrial workers, retailers, and others tends to dampen this kind of rivalry *within* the groups and to increase the opposition *between* groups—precisely where mutuality of interests should be emphasized.

In the healthy relation of people in society these two opposite aspects should be recognized. One is the mutual interests of complementary individuals, services, or material factors. The other is the rivalry between those that are essentially substitutes as, for example, one retailer can be a substitute for another. Both relations are valuable. In the judgment of this writer the former is more basic for it rests on the fact that a combination of factors is absolutely essential for production. No amount of labor can produce anything without capital, natural resources, direction, and the services of someone who brings these productive factors together. This is as basic and essential as the requirement of two parts of hydrogen and one part of oxygen to produce water. The other, i.e., competition, which is so useful in our system, could be dispensed with or minimized in certain other forms of society where authoritative control takes the place of free market forces.

So we conclude that the idea held by many that the essential relation of man to man is one of opposition and thus a basis for conflict deserves less emphasis than the opposite. This is a part of the philosophy of a free enterprise system though it is not commonly recognized. This is a reason that the concepts of struggle, war, and conflict are less emphasized in this philosophy and tolerance, mutual trust, and optimism somewhat more than in the opposite philosophy of a greater or less degree of authoritarian control.

In subscribing to this view of mutual interests of economic groups its adherents reveal another strand of thought. This is a willingness to take time enough for natural forces to work themselves out. They are not likely to make the mistake of killing the goose in order more quickly to get the golden eggs. This is logically a part of the liberal philosophy. It is also an aspect of conservatism. A conservative is usually a gradualist. So is a classic liberal because he is confident that nature and time are working together for good.

A proposition that recently appeared in an English book on industrial efficiency was that "we all live as we deserve." There is a good measure of truth in this but also a fallacy. We each live well or poorly, also because of the supply of other factors as we have said. But this also includes the "know how" and capital accumulated by earlier generations and passed on to us. We are all the heirs of the ages in the sense of advance of knowledge and civilization. More specifically, part of the supply of capital upon which American industry rests came directly or indirectly from the industry and thrift of our ancestors. In a short view, most of today's capital equipment has indeed been produced by this generation, but this has only been possible because industry of this generation has been very productive. This productivity was advanced by capital of a previous generation and that from a still earlier generation. Capital goods wear out and are replaced, but the social fund of capital which merely takes new physical forms is continuous. The difficulty of starting such a fund is a major problem of undeveloped countries.

This economic fact is another indication of the continuity of a society. It should make us less arrogant for our own accomplishments, more respectful for the contributions of our predecessors, and more sensitive to the duty we owe to our posterity.

Incidentally, these views are a central part of the conservative philosophy. It views "a people" as not merely constituting those now living. "The people" includes those who have gone before, those who are here now, and those who are to come. Obviously, a view of that kind encourages "conserving" of good things for the future. A policy that emphasizes this obligation is "conservative." If the good things it is trying to conserve are individual liberty and dignity, then it is both conservative and liberal in the logically correct use of the terms.

This awareness of the continuity of the life of the society, of what we derive from the past and what we owe to the future, affects the whole tone and overtones of conservative discussion. You will not often hear the quip from conservatives that we did often hear from the self-styled liberals in the thirties when some of their critics argued that some of the "shot in arm" remedies would have bad long-run effects. The supposedly devastating reply was, "In the long run we will all be dead." A conservative does not think this is funny. He recognizes that while we personally will be dead, the race, our nation or indeed our families will *not* be dead and the effects of our policies will be very much with them.

Capitalism the Equalizer

Another phase of the philosophy of a free society is that wide extremes of income and economic well-being are regarded as undesirable. This is true in spite of the fact that exponents of classical free enterprise would hardly be accused of egalitarianism. Equality is not emphasized so much by them as by the special advocates of "the masses" for the reason that, if carried too far, this equality clashes with the more basic belief that people should be rewarded in proportion to their contribution to the total product which certainly is not equal. The philosophy we are expounding does not look kindly upon any general program of taking from the rich to give to the poor. When, however, the poor are made more productive and for that reason come to enjoy larger rewards, the conflict of ideals is removed and this is a source of satisfaction. Precisely this has happened. As pointed out in stressing the mutual interests of economic groups, the position of the working classes, which constituted the lower economic group at the turn of the century, has been greatly improved, because of the increase in the other factors—especially capital, management, and enterprise. Not because of any special good will or altruism or indeed any conscious decision on the part of the possessors of these "other" factors, but by the sheer economic forces in a free competitive society, labor has become more valuable.

This, of course, is precisely the opposite of the view of Karl Marx. He never did grasp the truth and significance of marginal productivity applied to wages—which is, perhaps, not so strange, for the non-Socialist economists of his day had not grasped it either. But it is nevertheless a pity. For he did see and acknowledge the great contribution to output made by capital. What he missed was that the increase in output would increase the value of all the factors of production and particularly the scarce factors. Marx would probably have denied that labor would be scarce and Malthus, bemused by the supposed geometric rate of increase of the population, would have supported him. Be that as it may, he did predict the progressive "immiseration" of the proletariat and the increasing affluence of the capitalists, and thus a wider and wider gap between them. This was one of his great failures as a prophet.

There has been in the last 100 years a great leveling in the capitalistic world which can be best seen in the comparative consumption patterns and living standards of the upper and lower economic classes in this country and in others. An observation of these differences indicates that they are least in this most highly capitalistic country and greatest in underdeveloped countries. If we regard the countries of the world arranged even approximately in the order of their capitalistic development, with parts of Southeastern Asia at one end and Britain, Germany, and the United States at the other, it will be apparent that the contrast between the conditions of rich and poor declines quite consistently as we move toward the capitalistic end of the spectrum.

India is indeed a poor country, but some of the homes of the few large industrialists are more luxurious than those occupied by men of similar position in the United States. Beside these palatial houses, however, will be families who have no homes at all and are sleeping, cooking, and living in the streets.

By contrast, the difference in the United States in the way of life of the factory worker and of his employer is much less marked. The boss may have a ten-room house with three or four baths. The worker has a six-room house with one bath. Both have plumbing, hot and cold water, central heating, land for a garden, and garage or carport. The boss owns a Cadillac, a Lincoln, or an Imperial. The worker owns a Chevrolet or a Ford. The boss sends his son to a private school and an Ivy League college. The worker's boy goes to a public high school and perhaps to a state university. Regardless of bank account and investments, the difference in the actual way of life is surprisingly small. It is no doubt smaller than existed at most times in history.

It is quite common to explain this tendency to equality of real incomes on noneconomic or quasi-economic grounds. Not only is this explanation invoked by critics of a free enterprise system, who would naturally not like to concede this effect to pure capitalism, but even many defenders of capitalism like to call it the "new capitalism," "enlightened capitalism," "democratic capitalism" and so on. By these terms they refer to such measures as the progressive income tax, high inheritance taxes, public housing, development of labor unions, and general "welfare" legislation, as well as to the advanced sense of social responsibility of the capitalists.

How much the new pattern of income and consumption owes to these factors is hard to say. My own view is that their effect has been minor compared to the great economic forces of a growing capitalism. These forces are those discussed before in relation to the mutual interests of economic groups. There is no doubt at all that the startling advance in real wages in the past 50 years has come from improved technology, improved management, and increased capital per worker. These great forces are a natural outgrowth of comparatively free capitalism. By comparison the governmental and institutional measures mentioned above are mere gimmicks, which may help or may deter, but in either case cannot be the determinants of the greatest advance in economic wellbeing for a whole nation that the world has ever seen.

It is true we cannot prove that the technical advance, the improved management, and the accumulation of capital might not have come under some radically different economic system. But the fact is that it did come *under* capitalism and the relation of it *to* capitalism is more plausible than to any of the political devices of recent decades. This is not the place to engage in a lengthy defense of this proposition. It has been well argued by Professor Schumpeter in his *Capitalism, Socialism and Democracy,* particularly Chapters V to VIII. His argument may be more convincing to some readers, because it is part of a generally unfavorable prognosis for the future of capitalism. Like Marx, he predicts its downfall, but he has only the highest praise for its accomplishments as an economic system. And this is all I am asserting here—namely, that it is in the nature of capitalism to increase production and to reduce the gap between workers and owners. This justifies the characterization of "Capitalism the Equalizer." Not only is this proposition true as a matter of cold fact, but a faith in it is an element of the free enterprise philosophy.

The Affluent Society

Another corollary that flows from the philosophy of a free society is that an increase in abundance is good primarily because it enlarges the area of free choice of people. Let us recall this line of reasoning. The free society is one in which as many people as possible are as free as possible to seek the ends that to them seem good. To my mind, freedom in the strict sense is, as Professor Hayek says, absence of coercion. But the liberation of people is also advanced in a broader sense by an adequate supply of needed (or only desired) things. Affluence can advance their real freedom of choice, and hence it should be welcomed, not only for the direct satisfaction that flows from desired goods, but also because it is conducive to the growth of people as individuals.

Is there really any relation between the economic position of people and their own character, personality, and refinement? Certainly people in past ages have thought so. The Greeks, for example, took it for granted that the civilized person must have leisure for discussion and participation in noneconomic activities. In the Middle Ages it was assumed that it was only the upper classes that could possess civilization and culture. The peasant was supposed to be a clod, limited in his vision and appreciation of the finer things. It was such thoughts as these that were advanced to justify slavery, serfdom, or some other method of providing at least one class which was not completely absorbed in the task of eking out a miserable existence. It was not conceived that it would ever be possible to provide this easier life for the whole society. It required a high development of modern industry to bring that about.

In later years it has become fashionable to pretend that elevated tastes, cultural refinement, developed personalities, and high ethical standards are just as common among the poor as among the well-to-do. It would seem that a sensible judgment lies between these extremes. On the one side, very high incomes can encourage vulgar display and poor taste, but they can also lead to patronage of the arts, devotion to public service, or other worthy causes. In short, it makes possible a greater degree of freedom. Grinding poverty can and often does tend to create a narrow and mean life, though, of course, there are notable instances of individuals rising above this influence. But a condition in which the crude necessities are reasonably assured, in which reasonable comforts and occasional luxuries are quite within reach, gives a greater opportunity for growth and personal improvement.

Professor Galbraith in his *Affluent Society* is properly impressed by the great progress that has been made in this country in national product and in average incomes. From this fact he draws two important conclusions, the first being that the people of this country now have such substantial incomes that they have very few important unsatisfied wants and, secondly, that because of this abundance it has become necessary to "whip up" further demand by advertising and salesmanship. The argument runs that these artificially created demands are not very important anyway, and at the same time there are important needs in the "public sector." Hence we should divert purchasing power to these public needs. This is another way of saying that people have so much income that if left to their own free choice they will spend at least some of it in ways that would be less productive than those that the government would select.

The first of these two propositions is difficult to take seriously. Certainly there are very large numbers of people in the United States whose income could hardly be called affluent. These do not include only or even chiefly those who could properly be called poor. But there is the very large middle class or lower middle class for whom very real desires do not have to be whipped up by the arts of salesmanship. Professor Galbraith would only have to ask some of his teaching fellows or instructors if they could, offhand, think of things that they would like if their income were doubled. He would surely find in this category a number of things that are not heavily advertised. The other proposition seems to be that when the American people get beyond a certain level of income then any additional amounts can better be spent by the government for them than by themselves. The clash of this idea with the philosophy of a free society and of individualism is obvious, and this is the major objection of the classic liberal philosophy to the Galbraith thesis. If we do divert additional incomes to the public sector on the ground that has been given, it would be a denial of an opportunity that the human race now has for letting people live in their own way with a degree of freedom that has never existed before, and for giving them the opportunity to improve their standards of taste as a result of experience, education, and example.

Beyond such mundane matters is the freedom to make one's own choices between generosity and selfishness. We should not deny to people these opportunities by so diverting their purchasing power to an impersonal entity like the national state that they would not have the opportunity as individuals of making a choice at all. That the potentiality for freedom of choice is presented for the first time to so many people is the chief value of our increased affluence. In gaining this real freedom of choice a very important milestone in the history of the human race has been reached. In the philosophy of a free society it would be very unfortunate if this increased freedom were to be deliberately canceled out in favor of decisions made *for* people instead of *by* them.

Before leaving this subject we should add two comments. The first is that a reading of the *Affluent Society* suggests that to its author the desirable thing about the so-called "public sector" items is not the nature of the things or services, so much as that they are in the public sector. A number of them are, in fact, in both the public and private sectors and expansion in one is as possible as in the other. For example, privately-owned amusement places, toll roads, private hospitals, privately-owned universities, privately-supported drama and music. These have the advantage that free men support them as they desire them. Put the same things in the public sector and the freedom of choice of government is increased and that of individuals decreased.

Second, we should add that, of course, we do have needs for those items that in the nature of the case must fall in the public sector, e.g., courts, police, roads and so on, and a sensible community of responsible citizens will support programs of taxation necessary to provide these.

But the idea advanced by the exponents of the ever-expanding state goes far beyond this. The idea seems to be that there does not have to be a crying need for items in the public sector, because the money used for them would only be money that the public would use foolishly anyway or that perhaps the public would not be willing to spend at all.

In the latter eventuality it would be necessary for the government to expand its expenditures in order to keep the economy going. This latter variant goes back to the New Deal days when it was argued under the name of the mature economy theory, that we had gotten to a point where capital investment on a private basis would not be adequate to absorb the savings and that public expenditure was, therefore, essential to maintain full employment. This theory itself is a denial of the potentiality of a free enterprise society to maintain itself. The doctrine enjoys much less acceptance today than it did when it was first proposed in the 1930's. Perhaps it is not necessary for us to argue whether the theory is right or wrong, but it is significant for the purpose of this study, which is to identify the philosophy of a free society, to indicate that it stands in direct opposition to the theory of free enterprise. And free enterprise is the economic facet of a free society.

Freedom of Trade

In 1776 Adam Smith published his great book, *An Inquiry Into the Nature and Causes of the Wealth of Nations.* It was perhaps more than a coincidence that this was the year of our own Declaration of Independence. The former was a plea for economic freedom. The latter was a move for political freedom. The spirit of freedom was in the air, and that it should take these two forms is not surprising. The philosophy of a free society and of its economic aspect, freedom of enterprise, carries a compelling implication of freedom of trade, both within national boundaries and across them.

If men are to be free, it follows that they should be free to buy where they wish—as Adam Smith said to buy in the cheapest market and sell in the dearest market, a practice which he regarded as not only the natural right of people, but also a sound economic policy for a businessman or a nation. The principle is very broad and includes the freedom to buy or to sell at prices which are agreeable to the trading parties. The principle of free trade is violated when we engage in government price fixing or the establishment of "suggested manufacturers' prices" which involve a degree of coercion.

Free trade is the free working of the market without interference. One of the places where this interference has traditionally been most common is in the trade between the people of different nations. When Adam Smith was writing and in the period of two centuries before that time, the accepted idea was that a nation would become rich by regulating its trade with foreign countries in such a way as to influence the balance of trade in its favor. At that time this usually meant to gain an increase in the supply of gold in the country.

In later years the interference with the free flow of trade was more commonly undertaken for the purpose of restricting the competition of foreign sellers with domestic sellers, i.e., a protective tariff. A number of reasons were given for this policy, such as the development of industries (the infant industry argument) and a number of quite fallacious economic theories were advanced as to the effect of such a policy on the volume of employment. This is not the place to engage in an argument on the merits of free trade or protectionism. It is relevant, however, to note that the philosophy of a free enterprise society implies freedom of trade—a situation in which economic activities are regulated by the disciplinary forces of the market, rather than by the orders of authorities, private or public.

It may be remarked also that free trade in the international sense comes more naturally to a free-enterprise, privately-operated economy than to a Socialist economy. This is interesting because Marx and various others have emphasized the friendly relations that would naturally exist between Communist communities in contrast to the rivalry and striving for advantage that would characterize the capitalist societies. Certainly it is not true that the capitalistic societies would consistently refrain from use of protective tariffs. Quite the contrary. But it can fairly be said that the interference with competition represented by these tariffs is not logically a part of the free enterprise system. It comes as a surprise to some of us to see the number of instances in which statesmen and others, who in other respects are staunch advocates of a free enterprise system, find nothing inconsistent in advocating a protective tariff. That great political leader and spokesman for free enterprise, Senator Robert Taft, is a case in point. This is one example of the fact that it is rare that all the facets that would logically go together in a free enterprise system are, in fact, found in the same persons—particularly businessmen or men of public affairs.

But protectionism comes naturally to a Socialist system. Such a system frankly disavows the imperatives of a price system, which the Socialist is inclined to call the "haphazard decisions" of the market. It is a system of control, and so it is quite logical that its adherents should attempt to control trade of any kind, including trade across international boundaries. There is also a more specific reason for expecting a Socialist government to interfere in trade with foreign countries. Any dictator or government representative who desires to control the economy of a country must be ready to set prices and wages and determine the conditions of employment. These things he can perhaps do within some moderate limits if he confines himself to his own country, that is, to the area within which his orders will run. When, however, he ventures outside his controlled area he has no control over the prices which prevail there. He will quickly find that there is no appeal from the verdict of the world market, which gives precious little attention to his desires as to wages, prices and so on. This can be very frustrating, and a natural response is to say "let us free ourselves from this dependence upon the foreign market so that within our own boundaries we can control things according to our desires."[1] This is not only a theoretically probable reaction, but it was quite well demonstrated in England, which, during the nineteenth century, had become by precept and example a leader in the freeing of trade of the world. In the twentieth century, however, and particularly in the period between the wars, there was a growing tendency for the government to attempt to control the economy and to try by direct means to insure the welfare of the people of Britain. As this movement grew, the limitations mentioned a moment ago came into operation, and Britain moved from a free trade position over to protectionism. It also resorted to "empire preference" and other manipulations to try to maintain its position of leadership in the world at the same time that it was becoming more insular in its economic policies. The United States, on the other hand, during that period was expanding its overseas trade and foreign investments, and, under the leadership of Secretary Hull and others, we relaxed our protective tariff and accepted in international affairs the basic requirements imposed upon us by our own new economic position.

The fact seems to be then that a policy of free trade between nations is consistent with, and in fact is a part of, a philosophy of freedom of enterprise and is particularly consonant with a free world. The belief in a free enterprise system implies a belief in competition, and it is difficult to see why, if competition is so desirable within national lines, it is not also a good guiding force in the relation between nations. This we think is true in the sense of being economically advantageous to a coun-

[1] Of course, he may go farther and aspire to bring these recalcitrant foreigners under his political sway by conquest or less drastic political domination.

try. It, moreover, yields the kind of economic advantages which is consistent with the free enterprise philosophy, namely, that it is an advantage to all parties concerned, not one which is to be gained by one country at the expense of another. A basic assumption of this philosophy is that trade is not a swindle in which one party gains at the expense of the other. Trade is mutually profitable.

The economic advantage referred to was intended to cover the maximization of value received for the amount of effort and costs that were involved—in other words, economic advantage. Another closely related question is the effect of such a policy upon international relations in noneconomic ways. If it is true that trade is mutually advantageous, it should be a factor favoring peace. It is true that one group of sellers may be in rivalry with another group of sellers, and if these are from different nations they can involve economic rivalry between these nations, even to a point where efforts will be made to expand colonial territories and to gain advantages for the nationals of the different countries in investment and in selling. There is no doubt that this force did exist during the nineteenth century, and even more in earlier centuries. The trader, the pirate, and the armed forces were equal instruments for England in pushing its struggle against Spain in the sixteenth century. This concept of trade has not entirely disappeared today though it is much less common. This is an application of the competitive relationship in business, i.e., the relation of seller to seller; in this case, unfortunately, backed up by the sellers' governments.

But the more fundamental relation is that of buyer to seller. And in this relationship the outstanding feature is mutual advantage. Insofar as England was selling goods to Germany and Germany was selling goods to the United States or to England, there was a powerful influence for peace. That it was not strong enough to maintain the peace in two instances is attributable not to the influence of the businessmen, but to the influence of strong nationalists and war lords. Perhaps it is not going too far to include those who would like to expand the power of the state *within* its own boundaries. It is ironical that expanding the functions of the state to provide directly for the immediate welfare of the people should have the effect of creating a gulf between one nation and others. And this can well progress into actual conflict and the untold misery of those whose supposed welfare was the objective. Advocates of the welfare state reject this theory violently; indeed too violently to be convincing. It is a thesis that cannot be proven—it rests on logical deduction.

But historically it is interesting, at least, to observe that the hundred years from 1815 to 1914 was at the same time the most peaceful century the Western world has known and it was a century when much progress was made in *reducing* the power of the state. It came to an end after the turn of the century when the world began to move in the opposite direction.

It is statesmen and military men who make wars; the influence of businessmen in the relation of the great powers, at least in recent years, has been on the side of peace. Mr. Chamberlain, the Prime Minister of England, with his umbrella and his attempts to arrive at a peaceful solution with Hitler, is sometimes regarded as an amusing picture of the naive and ineffectual businessman in public affairs. Perhaps so, but his negotiations with Hitler represented a clash of two ideologies; one is that of the blustering, fanatical nationalist and the other of the grey, unromantic businessman. Chamberlain, the very prototype of the English businessman, simply could not understand how anyone would be willing to risk a war between two countries when it was quite evident that both of them would lose. The instinct of the businessman is to avoid the conflict, to accept compromise if necessary, not to worry too much about the principles involved, but to yield here and there what you have to yield and to get on with the business of the world. Such a person will never be pictured as a great hero. We could hardly visualize him with a plumed hat and riding a white horse, but he is the kind who is likely to keep the peace.

In 1913 Norman Angell wrote a book called *The Great Illusion.* The thesis of this book was on the lines just suggested. He argued that war had become an anachronism. Germany would surely not attack England because in doing so it would be attacking its good customers and blowing up its own assets and the same with England attacking Germany. It was true, incidentally, that for each of these countries the other was a more important market than any of those undeveloped countries whose favor they were both seeking. Since war was so obviously unprofitable it would not come.

The writer recalls the winning speech of a college oratorical contest in the spring of 1914 in which the Norman Angell theme was developed. Its peroration was that the intelligent self-interest of traders and businessmen will bring into effect the hopes of the ages, the promise of peace on earth, and good will among men. In less than three months the First World War came. The tragedy, of course, was that Norman Angell saw the peaceful forces of commerce and industry and did not pay sufficient attention to the age-old forces of political ambition and the various reasons for expanding the power of the state. It may be true that it is ideas that rule the world or throw it into chaos, but it was not the classic philosophy of liberalism that brought on that war or the Second World War: it was the archaic principles of the powerful state, which includes the welfare state and the planned economy. These are divisive forces. They do not provide the basis for a peaceful family of nations.

A Free System—A Force For Peace

One problem that might be raised about the free enterprise philosophy if not about our precise system, is the prospect of its being transplanted to other countries. If we look at the world outside the Communist bloc the evidence is certainly divided. And, of course, so it is as to Russia. However, within Russia itself one may expect changes growing out of its progress toward an industrialized society. As this process of industrialization goes on there are certain institutional changes that will almost inevitably follow.

It is interesting that one of the authorities to whom we could turn for this prediction is Karl Marx himself. The Marxian theory of materialism has been much misunderstood outside Communist circles. It is frequently taken to mean that the Communist cares only about material things and this is connected with atheism. But the meaning that Marx attached to it was that the forms of society would be dictated by the methods of production of material things. In other words, the requirements of the system of production of a society would determine its social form rather than the opposite. His application of this was that a certain form of society was normal when industry was in the handicraft state. When industry moved into a state of large plants and large numbers of workers, then another form was indicated and this was capitalism. But capitalism itself would produce even larger units and this trend and others would in turn lead to communism. We do not need to follow this theory to his conclusion in order to grant a certain degree of acceptance to the idea that the methods of production will have a bearing upon social organization or at least upon the industrial organization. And this is happening in Russia.

As the Russian economy has become more industrialized, the economic problems of allocating material and determining amounts of production of this and that has become more complicated. It has been almost inevitable that under these circumstances the authorities in the Kremlin would tend to place greater responsibility upon the local or regional managers. And so it has come about that the position of manager in a Russian industry more and more resembles the position of a manager of a local plant in one of our large corporations. A common characteristic of both is that the manager has gained a considerable freedom of decision and a large amount of responsibility is placed upon him. He, in turn, is likely to follow the same policy with his subordinates within his own plant. Insofar as this goes on, we get farther and farther away from the monolithic and highly centralized system. The problem of making automobiles in Russia cannot be essentially different than the problem of making automobiles in the United States or in any other country. There are certain requirements of the industry that simply must be met, regardless of ideology. Among these is a considerable diffusion of authority, which is a step toward freedom.

So we may expect as the process of industrialization goes on that the Russian industrial system will change. Some people have foreseen a convergence of the Russian system and our own. The implication usually is that the United States would move in some respects toward the Russian system, and Russia toward ours. On this particular matter of industrial organization, it seems more likely that the movement is to be made by them rather than by us. This does not reflect a mere bias in favor of our own system, but the fact that we are and have been an industrial country for some time. Our business system and a number of other features of our society have adjusted to this fact. The Russians are only now becoming industrialized, and it is only to be expected that the move to adjust their human organization of industry would be toward ours rather than ours toward theirs.

Another fact that may well influence Russia's economic and development organization is the wider range of choices which the consumers will presumably gain with their increased affluence. If the growing industry of Russia is turned more to consumer goods, as we may expect and as the leaders are now promising their people, this will give a greater freedom of choice to the people. For surely we cannot expect, if this abundance materializes, that they will simply produce and buy more of the things which they are now buying. They will presumably follow the same trend as has been apparent in the United States, that as purchasing power increases demand becomes more varied. As demand becomes more varied it becomes more difficult and indeed impossible to make the decisions as to volume of this or that, and for control of the distribution of these products from a central headquarters.

As long as the major problem in a country is whether the people are going to have shoes or not, there will be no great problem of market analysis to determine the particular style of shoes or colors or even the precise sizes of the shoes. But once you get past that original state, people are going to become more exacting about these details. It occurs to me that the job of a Russian commissar who is charged with the job of determining the color and other characteristics of lipsticks for the whole country would be a very uncomfortable one when the Russian girls generally begin to use them. It is a much simpler matter to decide that X percent of our resources are going to go to the production of steel than it is to determine how many of this type of lipstick is required and how many of the other, and how many should go to this community and how many to that. A system characterized by scarcity can be a centralized system; a system of affluence simply has to be decentralized. It must draw upon that special decentralized knowledge of time and place which plays such an important role in our enterprise system.

As to the industrial system itself, such changes as this seem to be quite clearly in the making. What bearing they will have upon the political ideology is another question. The problem has already occurred to the Russians, and some of their writers are now raising the question of how to maintain a collective spirit with increased affluence. Some of them are suggesting, for example, that as it becomes possible to have more automobiles, these will be organized into motor pools to be used collectively. Also it is suggested that increased recreation will not require individual cottages or hotels but will be provided by community resorts where several hundred or a thousand people will be sent for their vacations. To some of us a highly regimented scheme of that sort is quite repulsive. But apparently it is not so for all people. A very successful private enterprise exists in England organized by a Mr. Butlin for vacation spots for the masses, in which the activities of the day are completely organized. Apparently some people do like this and perhaps this will include the Russians. One recalls a humorous cartoon in which a little girl comes woefully to her mother and asks, "Mother, do I *have* to do just what I want to do?" Some people don't want to decide even what they want to do.

On the other hand, it can be argued that freedom is an indivisible sort of thing. If you are going to grant enough freedom in the field of production to draw upon the best individual initiative of managers and others in the plants, it is going to be very difficult to resist the tendencies toward individualism in other areas. The desire to make one's own choice in the purchase of goods and various other activities of life are likely to become more insistent. This will bear watching, but we can say that even today the Russian industrial system more nearly resembles ours than it does that of China. It is not inconceivable that within a few years the Russian political system and ideology will also move in that direction.

One must resist the temptation to extend this line of reasoning into an optimistic conclusion that there is a natural force bringing the world around to our ways. And one must resist this particular application of the economic interpretation of history. There are many potent forces outside the economic field which will have their effect. But it is encouraging to reflect that there is a certain logic in effective industrial organization which requires a degree of freedom on the part of a number of people. Or putting it another way, it requires many centers of decision. It may be that the Russians will be able so to compartmentalize the lives of their people that encouragement of the necessary individuality for effective industry can be confined to that area. It would not be surprising, however, to find that this is impossible, and that in the long run Marx may turn out to be correct in a way which he did not anticipate, in that this higher development of capitalism can only advance and be maintained in a general atmosphere of freedom and individuality.

This granting of freedom of thought and inquiry has been greatly extended by the Russians to their scientists and technicians. They have finally learned that a "deviationist" in physics or astronomy may be a pretty valuable man. Here again, can a scientist think freely and with daring in his field but be a conformist in sociology and politics? At any rate, the conceding of freedom as a requirement of progress by a people who were ideologically pointing in the opposite direction is the finest possible tribute to the central ideas of a free society and free enterprise.

A few years ago when I was in Japan a gentleman called upon me to remind me that he was a student of mine 40 years earlier and, with the Oriental's respect for his teacher, he had come to express his gratitude for all that the Americans had done for him. He had been in the United States as a boy for eight years, four years in high school and four years in college. He referred to the war experience and said that it was very difficult for him to live in Japan during that period, for he said once you have had that much exposure to American life you will almost inevitably think like an American. I was somewhat surprised at this comment and I asked him, suppose an American boy had lived in Japan for a corresponding number of years, would it be true that the Japanese way of thinking and their philosophy would likewise be impressed upon him? His answer was very positive that, with all respect to Japanese philosophy and values for the Japanese, there was no question in his mind that the American ideas with their greater emphasis on freedom were more exportable than theirs. We may hope that this is true.

XIII.

CONCLUSION

Is a Free Market System New or Old?

The doctrine which has been expressed in this study may well be called both by its friends and its enemies old-fashioned. The opposing doctrine of the planned economy and a high degree of control of economic activities by the state is often regarded as new. It is referred to as the "wave of the future," "the brave new world," and the "application of science to social problems." But which of these is old and which new depends upon the point of view. If one is viewing this question in the perspective of the whole history of the race or of Western civilization, let us say, from 400 B.C. in Greece through Rome and Western Europe down to the present time, a much better case can be made for calling the free market system new. For throughout this whole period it was assumed that the state or other authorities should exercise control over the economy. For the most part these economic controls were exercised in relatively small areas such as duchies, principalities, guilds of European towns, and the feudal estates. But sometimes the controls extended over very large areas as, for example, the efforts of Diocletian to control prices and wages in the Roman Empire, the efforts of the merchant leagues like the Hanseatic League to regulate trade in the later Middle Ages, and the effort in early modern times to control the domestic economy in most of the European countries, but most notably in France by Colbert acting for Louis XIV. Under various forms and devices these were all expressions of the idea of centralized control of human activities. That these things had to be controlled seemed obvious. In France in 1718, for example, it was discovered that government control had somehow overlooked the cloth industry in the town of Langogne. An edict was published stating that, "His Majesty is informed that no reglement specifies from how many threads those cloths are to be composed; *a matter which must be attended to without fail*."[1]

These efforts met with more or less success, more success indeed when the economic conditions of the area being governed were relatively simple as in an agricultural economy and less successful in the presence of a growing and active commerce. (The reglements just mentioned broke down in the face of growing industry. They just would not work.) But as far as the age of the two ideas is concerned there is not a bit of doubt that the control idea was the old one, that it was necessary to dispense with these controls and to rely upon what Adam Smith called the free and natural system of liberty before the industrial revolution and the great expansion of trade could take place. The modern age brought with it freedom of the market. This was a free enterprise system, imperfect it is true, but basically different from what we had had before in that the primary directive forces were those of an impersonal price system.

The effect was to increase the freedom of men—of all men but particularly of the enterprisers who initiated and conducted the economic affairs of the society. It was under this philosophy that the great expansion of the nineteenth century took place. It was only as we got into the twentieth century that there was more and more attempt to use the power of the state to accomplish certain ends. Without arguing, for the moment, whether these ends were desirable or not or whether it was an effective way of obtaining them, there can be no question that the

[1] On this whole subject of government regulation see the classic work of Eli F. Heckscher, *Mercantilism*.

changes in direction in the twentieth century represented a reversion to the age-old approach to human problems which had been rejected only a short time before. Authoritative control is as old as the hills; the free market only reached its height in the last century. Socialism, communism, and planned economy are only new words for age-old authoritative organization.

Of course, if one wants to disregard the history of twenty-five hundred years and think merely of the nineteenth century compared to our present years, there would be some justification for calling this present-day trend to big government new. It is new compared to yesterday, but in reference to the long sweep of history it is a reversion to an old and discredited philosophy. Partly the confusion arises from the desires of adherents of a variety of present-day systems to stress the differences between them. There are, of course, differences between fascism, communism, and "democratic socialism," but in any comparison with a free system, their basic similarity overshadows their differences.

Social systems break down into two forms, namely, the systems that place primary responsibility upon the individuals and rely upon an automatic disciplinary force of the market, on the one side and those that attempt to control the system consciously on the other. True, there are many ways of classifying societies but this one seems quite fundamental for it is an aspect of man vs. society or individual vs. group, a very old and pervasive question.

Accomplishments of Liberalism

It has become fashionable in many quarters to disparage the past in favor of our "brave new world." Particularly the nineteenth century has been thus treated. It has been scornfully called the "horse-and-buggy age" and an age of "crass materialism." Let us see. During the century, the liberal ideology prevailed in the countries which were, in fact, the leaders and whose policies were profoundly influencing the whole world. During that period, the world enjoyed a material prosperity which, in its absolute level, had never been attained before and which exceeded all earlier periods in its rate of progress. It would be difficult to give any reliable figures that would measure this productivity for the whole world, but the effect of it was reflected in increased population. During that period it is estimated that the population of the world doubled; the population of western continental Europe trebled; the population of Great Britain quadrupled; and the population of the United States increased some twentyfold.

It is a matter of common observation that this larger number of people enjoyed a higher standard of living than existed in previous centuries. That improvement was very marked in the industrialized countries, but through the influence of trade and, hence, the possibility of each country's specializing in its most effective lines, the improvement of living standards extended to the whole world. The improvement was to be measured not merely in terms of a better supply of such basic items as food, which, of course, was reflected in the larger population, but also in the manufacture of many utterly new products and the improvement in the quality of other products. In short, on the material side, many more people were supported at higher standards of living.

Nor should this improvement be discounted as merely material, for the raising of standards above bare subsistence made possible improvements in other aspects of life which may be considered much more important. For several countries as a whole and for large masses of people in other countries, the fear of famine and starvation was abolished. In view of the fact that these two had always been among the major scourges of mankind, this was no mean accomplishment.

Beginning with the late eighteenth century and extending through the nineteenth century, there was also a great extension of freedom in several of its aspects. There was the growth of political self government in the older countries; the firm establishment of the United States as a free country; and the development in it of democratic institutions. The century saw the abolition of slavery and the disappearance of serfdom in the Western world. There was also the abolition of many restrictions upon the free movement of workers from one occupation to another and from place to place within the world. The large migration to the United States was an example, as was our own occupation of our West.

Public education was established during this period and brought with it a revolutionary change in the degree of literacy. The higher institutions of learning also prospered, both with private and public support. While there is little evidence that the best educated people of 1900 were markedly superior in wisdom and broad culture to those of 1800, it is clearly true that many more people were educated at both the elementary and higher levels.

In international relations it was a period of increasingly free contacts. On the material side, the policy of free trade developed and indeed extended so far that by the middle of the century it was possible for Cobden, the great free trade statesman of England, to say that he considered the extension of free trade to the whole world to be as sure as the rising of tomorrow's sun. This extension of free trade, which was generally accepted as an ideal even by those who defended protectionism for various temporary or special reasons, was a reflection of the growing feeling of educated people that they were citizens of the world. This genuine internationalism was apparent in many ways. The Russian composer, Tschaikovsky, and the Polish composer, Chopin, were as much at home in Paris as in their own countries. The culture of the world, which to a considerable extent was European culture, was not nationalistic. There was, in short, a free trade in ideas and ideologies which matched the free trade in goods. These extensions of cultural contacts came naturally as an expression of the spirit of the times.

We are today striving to create such contacts in artificial ways with associations and foundations and with a special assistant secretary of the Department of State in charge of cultural relations. These activities, although they can be commended in view of the conditions that face us, are a poor substitute for a spontaneous and natural sharing of cultures. The expression "one world" was coined by Wendell Willkie, tragically enough after the tide had turned toward a disintegration of world civilization. We were closer to attainment of one world in the nineteenth century than we have been since that time.

The policies of statesmen and diplomats, although serving the interests of their nations, were in that century largely directed to the maintenance of peace. If this be doubted, it should be borne in mind that the ideal of international peace was largely a development of the eighteenth and nineteenth centuries, corresponding almost precisely with the development of liberal ideals. Prior to that time it was considered, even by such men as Grotius, that war—or at least an attitude of war—was the normal relationship of nations.

Moreover, in the actual record, if we can consider for a moment the nineteenth century as extending from the end of the Napoleonic Wars in 1815 to the outbreak of World War I in 1914, this was in fact the most peaceful century that Western civilization has known since the fifteenth century and before that the Pax Romana of the early Roman Empire. This conclusion is based upon quantitative studies which measure the extent of wars by the number of them, the number of participants, the number of casualties, the number of countries involved, and the proportion of combatants to the total population. By comparison, the two centuries preceding the nineteenth and, even more, the twentieth century following, make a very poor showing. Not only were actual conflicts at a low level during the nineteenth century, but statesmen, and educated people generally had come by the end of that one-hundred-year period to regard war between great states in the civilized world as an anachronism. This optimistic attitude and vision of the future was expressed by Tennyson, the poet laureate of England:

> Yet I doubt not through the ages one increasing purpose runs,
> And the thoughts of men are widened with the process of the suns
> Till the war drum throbs no longer, and the battle flags are furled
> In the Parliament of man, the Federation of the world.

As with the attitude toward war, so in other fields the prevailing spirit of this period was the growing optimism which regarded the injustices and flaws of the actual world as but temporary imperfections which surely reasonable men in succeeding generations would remove. The pessimism as to the future of Western civilization—indeed, the future of *any* real civilization—and the recurring contemplation of the "next war" are developments of the twentieth century.

These things are said not in a spirit of nostalgia, but to suggest that in any sober evaluation of what we have accomplished in the first half of this century we should not be vainglorious, nor should we forget the contributions which our forebears made toward human freedom and dignity. We might also consider that the liberal philosophy of that century was intimately tied into these aspects of progress. Men of the twentieth century with all their self-conscious planning for welfare through the state will do well if they match in fundamentals the performance of the nineteenth century. If they are going to do so, they had better get on their way, for time is running out.

Decline of Liberalism

But toward the end of the nineteenth century and in the early twentieth century, there appeared a significant change in social philosophy. Some would call it an improvement upon traditional liberalism. Whether an improvement or not, it was a departure from the fundamental tenets of that philosophy. The manifestations, on the practical side, were an expansion of the functions of the state and, on the ideological side, a shift in emphasis to an abstract "social" welfare and away from the rights, freedoms, and opportunities of specific flesh and blood individuals. This shift of emphasis naturally encouraged group action to attain reforms and to bring the abundant life. The increased reliance upon group action and upon the power which such groups could exert led some people to favor schemes of state socialism and others to favor communism and the dictatorship of the proletariat. Outside Russia and its satellites most people of Western civilization did not go to these extremes; but they did accept as an objective of the state the actual welfare of its citizens, not merely the provision of an environment in which they could seek their own welfare.

To those taking this moderate view it appeared that one of the most obvious ways in which the state could directly advance the welfare of its citizens was to grant privileges to groups. This movement we have called "groupism," as distinguished from "statism." How this acted to impair the discipline of the market has already been mentioned. A common characteristic of this approach through functional groups is that it visualized gains to one group at the expense of others. It thus leads to restraints upon or softening of the competition impinging upon the favored group. This represents a reversal of the philosophy of classic liberalism.

Another symptom of a decline in liberal attitudes in the classic sense is in the popularity and implications of the term "economic planning." This term came into popularity during the thirties, although the roots of the idea go far back of that time. There were indications of the growth of this idea in intellectual circles in the last two decades of the nineteenth century in this country, and there was a substantial growth of it in Europe, particularly in Germany, even before that time. In that country great social welfare schemes were promoted by the Prussian bureaucracy.

A considerable group of young American economists went to Germany for study and many of them were greatly attracted by this program and the philosophy that underlay it. These young men, as they returned to academic positions in this country, greatly influenced economic thinking, at least in academic circles. The teaching of economic science in the United States up to that time was largely a continuation of the classical school of England—Smith, Mathus, Ricardo, James Mill, and others. At this time, specifically the late 1880s the trek to Germany began. Its influence favorable to regulation of industry, mild state socialism, and welfare economics spread widely in American universities.[2]

[2] One of the leaders of this young group was Richard T. Ely, who, upon his return, was appointed to The Johns Hopkins University, where he headed a seminar of some 12 young men for and by whom the new concept of the relation of the state to the economy was propounded. This small group included Woodrow Wilson; Albion Small, later dean of the University of Chicago; John R. Commons, who greatly influenced the so-called liberal program in Wisconsin and its exponent, Senator La Follette; Henry Carter Adams, chairman of economics at the University of Michigan; Boise Penrose, later Senator, and others. Ely and his group also were instrumental in starting the American Economic Association and its journal, *American Economic Review*. It seems fair to say that the influence of Ely and the others was toward German state socialist ideas and away from English classical and neo-classical economics. They gave an intellectual foundation for the new brand of liberalism.

But up to the early thirties the practical influence of the new economics upon statesmen was largely confined to reforms in this field or that, most of which were not inconsistent with a reasonable interpretation of the liberal philosophy. Among these reforms were limitations on child labor, workmen's compensation acts, public regulation of natural monopolies, and others which were sponsored by Theodore Roosevelt and the Progressive party and by Woodrow Wilson under his banner of the "New Freedom." Indeed, even the "New Deal," as the term was used by Franklin Roosevelt in his first campaign for the presidency, covered a variety of reforms which most progressive thinkers endorsed. It did not imply a unified program, and the term "economic planning" was not used. As the depression continued, however, the idea arose that a comprehensive plan of action was necessary to cope with it.

Another root of this idea is no doubt in the comprehensive planning on the part of large American business firms. In their case, great and comprehensive plans were laid, organizations were set up to carry them through, and all this activity excited the admiration of the world. It seemed but natural to expect that if American businessmen could do these things effectively the same American genius should be able to solve our great economic problems. On more than one occasion in our history, when we were faced by a critical situation, there has come this demand for the leadership of businessmen, and the use of business methods and organizations. To meet the crisis of depression it was proposed by business leaders, prominent among them Gerard Swope of the General Electric Company, that leaders of business, labor, and agriculture should combine their efforts to solve the great problem. Enlisted in support of this ideal was also a very different group of people, those who favored reforms of an egalitarian nature. And another group were those in business, agriculture, and labor who sought relief from the rigors of competition. Their ideas were expressed in the N.I.R.A. (National Industrial Recovery Act). From these varied sources, then—Prussian bureaucracy and state socialism in Europe, the indigenous reform movement in this country, the large-scale planning and execution of plans by American business, the desire to escape from competition, and the aspirations of egalitarian reformers—there arose the concept of economic planning.

This concept differs from earlier reform movements in several ways. One is that certain broad objectives, particularly those having to do with the distribution of wealth and the maintenance of full employment, should be accepted as goals and as responsibilities of the government and that deliberate and extensive plans should be drawn for realizing them. Broadly speaking, the earlier reformers had relied upon changing certain institutions and laws as, for example, in the case of the workmen's compensation acts which provided a basis of compensation for injuries more realistic than the old common law rules—in other words, modifying at one point or another the rules of the game. The ideal of economic planning, on the other hand, involved the increase of administrative power and a more direct approach to desired ends. The analogy of a country at war was often used to express this ideal, for in wartime a more or less concerted and organized program is set up for the economy. Why not, it was asked, use such a program to solve peacetime problems? This approach appealed to many people who were attracted by Socialist ideals of an orderly society but who were not willing to go all the way with the Socialists. The fact that the objective in war is simple, overpowering, and presumably universally accepted, but that this was quite different from the multitude of objectives of a nation of free people was not recognized by these advocates of planning.

Another concept closely related to economic planning—indeed, implicit in it—is the idea of the welfare state. The essence of this idea is that the state is responsible for the welfare of its people, not merely for so governing them that they may seek their welfare. The Declaration of Independence referred to life, liberty, and the *pursuit* of happiness. At one time it was regarded as humorous that some careless draftsman, in drawing up the constitution for one of the states, omitted the words "pursuit of" from the famous phrase, so that the inalienable rights asserted by the Declaration included happiness itself. But under the modern concept of the state in relation to its citizens, that broad statement would apparently be accepted in all seriousness by some people.

Of course, there are a number of implications in this view. The concept of the "general will" comes into play. If the state is responsible for the welfare of the people, it must decide what that welfare consists of. Moreover, it must *act* to assure that welfare. This calls for the use of force in one form or another. Dissenting minorities must be overridden. Government, i.e., political parties, must be allowed some continuity of control to carry out these programs. So the logic of the welfare state extends to degrees of control and kinds of government of which the sponsors perhaps never dreamed.

Whatever one may think of these different ideologies, the fact is apparent that the world presents a very different picture today from that which was envisaged by the philosophers and leaders of traditional liberalism. Even in this country, which probably has resisted the retreat from classical liberalism more than others, the role of the state has tremendously increased until something like one-third of the national income is spent by various governmental units. To a degree undreamed of in the past, occupational groups, labor, farmers, and others have attained power, for better or for worse, to control their individual members and to impose their will upon other members of the society.

Why did a policy and a philosophy that seemed so well established and gave so much promise decline in such a short time? It is as impossible to give a complete explanation for this change as it is to give a completely satisfactory explanation of the rise of liberalism in the first place. But a number of points may be noted.

In the early days of our country a potent check to the extension of government powers and to any infringement through organized group action upon the rights of individuals existed in the memories of the struggle for the freedoms recently gained. But the very success of the liberal policies of the late eighteenth and nineteenth centuries had established civil rights and economic freedom so well that many people come to accept them as a matter of course and thus to regard them in the same class as sunshine, fresh air, and other free goods. But people are not solicitous and careful about their free goods, and the preservation of them does not determine people's actions. So it is with social blessings which are taken for granted. This does not necessarily mean that people in the Western countries place a low value upon their liberties. Rather, the effect has been to lull us into a feeling that, except for such obvious threats as those of a foreign enemy, a subversive antidemocratic group within our borders, or a would-be dictator, all will be well. The more insidious erosion of property rights and the rights of individual workers and others caused by well-meant reforms does not today cause the alarm to us that they would have caused to our forefathers. This change in mass psychology is favorable to the extension of group powers.

It may also be that such a high ideal as liberalism required the support of a formal religion which emphasized the importance and dignity of individual men. The force of formal religion is probably less today than it was a century ago. Indeed, the ideals of liberalism have fostered and encouraged rational inquiry and the scientific attitude which, in spite of its many values, has helped to undermine religion. The result has been that in place of the will of God we are glorifying the will of the majority. And the place of Providence in men's minds is being usurped by the providential state. These trends have gone far in some other countries. But evidences of this trend in ideology are not entirely absent in our own country.

Then there has developed a yearning for security. In the preceding centuries men were born to or assigned to classes in society, and their rights and welfare were largely determined by this status. A feature of liberalism has been to break down the security which such arrangements implied. The rate of change, technologically and in other respects, in the last 150 years has been terrific. One writer has called it a perpetual gale. Just as a child may, after a brief freedom, want to return to the greater security of his parental home, so Western people have a yearning for security, even if it means less freedom. While some thinkers frankly assert that freedom or security is the choice, more people believe we can enhance both freedom and security. In one sense of the term "security," that is possible. For if in a free society the level of production is high and the economy is expanding, opportunities will be great, and those conditions in themselves will provide genuine security.

But to many people, security means more than an improved chance to strive. To them it means the *assurance* of good things regardless of effort and the prudent direction of it. Security for all, in that sense, is an illusion, for if the total environment is changing, as it must change if we are to have progress, then the guarantee of security to anyone or to any one group must increase uncertainty for the others. If, for example, the rate and character of change means that there is a real possibility that the national income may drop by 25 percent and if certain groups have been able so to entrench themselves through rigid wages or prices that their own incomes would only suffer by 10 percent, the result will be that others must take a reduced income of *more* than 25 percent. The stability of one group in an unstable society can, generally, be attained only at the expense of exaggerated insecurity to others.

Another explanation for the tendency to conscious and centralized control is the fact that a number of industries are of such a nature as to make the operation of competition in greater or less degree impractical. These we have come to recognize as public utilities; and, since for them the normal regulative forces of competition do not suffice, the public demands that they be regulated as to rates and quality of service and equality of treatment of consumers. Toward the end of the nineteenth century and increasingly since that time, these controls have been extended. As control of rates and other features of business have been applied in greater degrees and to more industries, the possibility of free competition has been reduced even farther than the natural forces would have dictated. This, it can be argued, calls for a continuance of regulation. The extension of regulation and of the public utility concept is thus unfortunately cumulative.

One aspect of this cumulative effect is that the setting of rules and rates which at first are resisted by an industry may soon be recognized as the most effective way of restricting competition. Such regulation may have the effect of protecting the consumer, but it also (as, for example, in the trucking industry) protects established firms from the casual, sporadic competition of individual truckers. In this way government regulation sometimes does for the established firms what they could not do themselves, because of natural economic forces or perhaps because of the Sherman Antitrust Act. Thus the regulated first tolerate and then embrace the limitations on their own freedom. Who then is left to resist the trend? Not the consumers, for the only protection they know is the regulating commission. Not the companies, for regulation does for them what the Sherman Act would prohibit if attempted by themselves. About the only likely objectors are the potential competitors who might enter the business if they could do so at their own prices. But, since we do not even know who they are, their political influence is minimal.

The extension of control in the public utility field has induced in many people an exaggerated view of the need and possibility for the same type of control in other fields, not in the natural monopoly category. We even hear the suggestion that any large company should be treated as a public utility with its prices determined as are railroad rates.

Outside the field of public utilities and others where natural monopolies exist, there has been a change in the nature of competition. To this change people have reacted differently. There is one group which, while recognizing that there has been some change in the nature and forms of competition, believes that the new competition is even more socially useful than the old. But there is another group which feels that the change represents a decline of competition and that this decline has gone too far to be checked. They would accept that fact, substitute for competition more extensive regulation of the economy, and thus would move away from the true liberal system. In some countries this last group has very great force, and, indeed, in this country at times it has enjoyed powerful sponsorship. The view is closely allied to that of the socialist who denies not only the practical possibility but also the theoretical desirability of competition.

In contrast to these shifts in ideology, there have been certain very practical forces which have led to the extension of the power of the state. The most important of these forces have been the two great world wars, in which this country and most of Western civilization have been involved in the twentieth century. In many respects the most potent enemy of the liberal way of life is war. For war leaves little room for the individual aspirations of men and demands that the actions of all shall be bent to a single national purpose. We can, however, inject into this rather gloomy picture of the decline of the liberal idea the observation that the American people accepted the wartime restrictions only as temporary expedients and they tore up their ration books with great glee at the end of the war. But still some of the wartime controls did remain.

A group of more lasting pressures are those created by a great depression. During such a period the problems that affect everyone are or seem to be created by great social and economic forces with which the individual is powerless to cope. Like a war, therefore, a depression encourages the extension of governmental powers, and perhaps still worse, it leads to the establishment and strengthening of private power groups.

As we remarked in our first explanation of the decline of liberalism, people tend to become careless of blessings which they have merely inherited. This complacency induced in the minds of many people the view that the struggle for freedom had been won. This view was expressed by writers in the latter part of the nineteenth century like Herbert Spencer for example, in the conclusion that the progress of all the ages had culminated in this best of all possible worlds.

Such a philosophy naturally provided a support for those individuals and classes who still enjoyed privileges and for their very natural attitude of extreme conservatism and "standpatism." But this was a distortion of the philosophy of liberalism. The needs for reform were real as they always will be. Instead of relying upon the only partially realized ideals of liberalism, the humanitarians and especially the young reformers turned to an opposite philosophy. We are thus, in the words of Walter Lippmann, "a generation that has lost its way." It is fortunate that there has been no diminution in the desire for reform; but partly because of the opposition of many of those who falsely carried the banner of liberalism, the reform spirit struck off in new and strange lines. In this view the vehicle of mankind was proceeding during the nineteenth century along the right road toward an extension of human freedom. For a number of reasons, some of which we have indicated, it became stalled. The real problem was for young reformers to get it started again on that road. Instead, many of them took a bypass, a short cut, which, in the opinions of some of us, leads back to the bottom of the long hill which the human race must climb if freedom is to be maximized.

The view that progress lies along a road, which was indicated by social philosophers and statesmen of the past one-and-a-half centuries, is expressed in the term "liberal-conservative." If this hyphenation appears to be a contradiction in terms or a milk-and-water halfway position, it is because in popular usage "liberal" has come to mean "new," and "conservative" a defense of "status-quo." But that is, as we have argued, a superficial interpretation of the terms. The liberal philosophy is the timeless and fairly definite body of concepts which we have tried to explain. It has a set of ideals which are far from realized. One who is attached to these ideals will try to preserve them, i.e., *conserve* them, and thus is a conservative as well as a liberal.

A Positive Program of Liberalism

In a way the liberal program as it touches on government is negative. It is said that when the king of France asked one of the physiocrats, who were in some respect forerunners of Adam Smith's doctrine of the free market, "What do I need to do to make my country prosperous?" the reply was "laissez faire, laissez passer," let them (the people) do what they please. Or, as one report goes, the king was advised to go and play tennis and leave the country alone. This advice of noninterference was probably salutary when considered against the almost unbelievable maze of regulations that was hampering the trade and industry of the country under mercantilism. But as a well-balanced and permanent policy it will not do. Freedom does not thrive under anarchy. A high level of statecraft is required to organize and preserve a liberal society. Surely not as many directives as in a planned economy are required, but there will be equally important basic rules of the game.

The classic liberal does not subscribe to the crude laissez-faire doctrine that that government is best which governs least.[3] The preservation of a competitive system requires rules just as a highly competitive football game requires a book of rules and several officials to oversee a game.

Can we here suggest certain features of a positive program of liberalism? It is a risky thing to attempt because many people who may subscribe to a body of general principles may well disagree on specifics. This is as it should be. The most that should be hoped for is acceptance of some basic conceptions and goals. In this spirit we shall suggest some problems and broadly some positions that seem to this writer consistent in the modern world with the classic philosophy of a free society.

First, a positive program of liberalism should include vigilance to preserve the elements of freedom to people of all kinds and classes. This includes vigilance against possible infringement of individual rights by the government itself. If there is an advance in prices in the steel industry we should at least carefully weigh the danger of inflation against the long-run consequences of a display of extra legal power of the national government to interfere with the working of the market.

It also refers to preserving rights of people against infringement by other people or groups of people. This obligation of government is particularly difficult to meet wisely because making any changes that increase the rights of one citizen may take something away from another. For this reason it is desirable that as far as possible the establishing of new rights and duties should come from mutual consent of the parties as they do in the marketplace. Of course, the liberal would prefer to avoid governmental coercion in favor of education, example,

---

[3] A statement of this need for political action in the liberal scheme is provided by Sir Andrew McFadyean in the *Encyclopedia Britannica*. As a political leader Sir Andrew perhaps overstresses the need for expanding the role of the state but in our view he is quite right in distinguishing between classic liberalism and laissez faire. He writes as follows:

"Liberalism is a belief in the value of human personality, and a conviction that the source of all progress lies in the free exercise of individual energy; it produces an eagerness to emancipate all individuals or groups so that they may freely exercise their powers, so far as this can be done without injury to others; and it therefore involves a readiness to use the power of the state for the purpose of creating the conditions within which individual energy can thrive, of preventing all abuses of power, of affording to every citizen the means of acquiring mastery of his own capacities, and of establishing a real equality of opportunity for all. These aims are compatible with a very active policy of social reorganization, involving a great enlargement of the functions of the state. They are not compatible with socialism, which, strictly interpreted, would banish free individual initiative and responsibility from the economic sphere."

and moral suasion. Where government determination becomes necessary, the liberal philosophy would favor the use of the power of government in as small geographic areas as is feasible, for the reasons mentioned in our discussion of federalism.

Second, there should be a policy of holding in check the power of coercion by private persons or groups. Coercion should be the monopoly of the state, which in a liberal and democratic society should use it cautiously, carefully, and economically. The most serious indictment to be brought against the modern brand of liberalism in this country, and specifically against some aspects of the New Deal, is not that it expanded the basic power of the state. In a sense the fair criticism is just the opposite, namely, that it increased the power of private groups and transferred the power of coercion, which should be the final and overpowering weapon of the state itself, to private organized groups. Through the encouragement and exemption from prosecution of those private groups, this policy violated the principle that any state must observe if the rights of individuals are to be preserved. An example is the tolerance of mass picketing and violence by some labor unions. The fact that liberalism would keep the functions of the state at a low level does not imply a weakening of the state or an impairment of the majesty of law. It does hold that law will retain its majesty, first, as long as it is based upon principles that are universally applied and, second, as long as the sovereignty of the state shall be used sparingly. The actual use of power should be slight; the reserve of power in the state should be great and unquestioned.

A third major objective related to this one should be the preservation of competition. It is clear enough that a condition of competition does not maintain itself automatically. Altogether too frequently competitors do not like competition. Competition is one of those concepts which most thoughtful businessmen and workers recognize and admire in the abstract; but in the concrete and specific instances, they are frequently ready to limit it. That is the very reason why the state should act to preserve competition. For it can be stated as a general principle of government that a function of the state is to enforce those principles upon which we generally agree but which some individuals are willing to violate. If there is not general agreement on the principle, the rule will not be enforceable; if there is not the tendency to violate it, there is no need of enforcement.

It is not, therefore, an exaggeration to say that in a democracy the major economic function of government should be to preserve competition among the members of the society, for it is the system of checks and balances in our economic system that directs activities of individuals into lines acceptable to society, without the use of force. As Professor Henry Simons wrote, "A nation that is not willing to submit to the discipline of competition will ultimately find itself under the discipline of authority."

This function of government has been recognized in the field of business by our antitrust laws. But, outside the area of business, government in recent years has been following a strangely contradictory policy as to other groups—such as independent retailers, farmers, workers, and professional associations— so that it frequently appears not as the guardian of competition but as the sponsor of monopoly.

A liberal program will support and vigorously enforce these laws. There are pitfalls to be avoided. These laws which were designed to preserve competition should not be misdirected to the preservation of competitors. This objective leads to protecting some from the force of competition. Another danger is that the law against monopolizing may be used for an indiscriminate attack upon bigness, prompted not by any real desire to *preserve* competition, but by a desire of smaller firms to *avoid* competition. These instances indicate that a liberal policy is not insured by the passage of good laws, but requires constant care in their administration to see that their spirit and purpose are observed. Probably a liberal policy will not exist without a liberal philosophy which permeates all agencies of government and the general public too.

Fourth, there are certain problems that the adherents of traditional liberalism have been too willing to leave simply to natural forces. Among these is the problem of individual security. This problem, viewed in its broadest aspects, is the most difficult one to reconcile with the ideals of a free society. The reason is that the ideal of freedom is that each individual shall have the opportunity to advance his interests, as he may define them in the way that seems best to him, as long as he does not infringe upon the liberties of others to do the same thing. But the freedom to seek one's self-defined interests in one's own way implies that one must have the freedom to make foolish decisions as well as wise ones, and these foolish decisions or mere lethargy may well lead to individual disaster. That is the price of freedom. The desire for security, on the one hand, is the desire to protect people from such misfortunes. Thus is posed the basic problem of how to avoid or compensate for the disasters that may accompany freedom without impairing the freedom itself.

It is not too difficult to attain a high degree of security if that is all we seek. For example, a society dominated by status would provide at the same time a low degree of opportunity and a high degree of security. Moreover, the very hope of providing rising levels of security for all depends upon industrial progress. But progress of any kind implies change and, to a considerable extent, unpredictable change. That being true, the ideals of progress and security are incompatible in the short run and in the view of individuals adversely affected by the changes.

We must, however, recognize that individuals have both of these desires: the desire for improvement and the desire for security; and, therefore, in a good society dominated by liberal principles a compromise must be sought. The first line of attack upon the problem of security can be to establish certain "floors" or minima below which levels the incomes and economic well-being of people should not be allowed to decline despite vicissitudes or the people's own foolishness. The competitive ideal in its unadulterated form is too rigorous to commend itself to people of humanitarian impulses, and it is well that that should be true. For a society in which the weak would be allowed merely to fall by the wayside is shocking to our better natures. Moreover, if that harsh policy is followed to extreme limits we could well lose the values of mutual aid which are necessary to a strong society.

The problem of providing such minimum incomes and of still retaining the essentials of a competitive system is a difficult one. It involves the question of how much the society can afford, which is largely a question of productivity. It also raises the question of how to avoid a dulling of incentives. It is an unpleasant but nevertheless a real fact that for many people any reasonable minimum will be gladly accepted in place of effort for something more. It is a further unpleasant fact that the group that is likely to need help includes a disproportionate number of undermotivated, or shall we plainly say, lazy, people. Of course it also includes many deserving unfortunates. But it is the others that create the problem of how to give help without destroying incentives.

A third but related problem is to avoid a distortion of the price system upon which a healthy free enterprise economy rests. For example, a minimum wage may be sponsored by those who desire to improve the lot of workers. But if a minimum is set high enough to have any appreciable effect it can very well create unemployment. The reason is very simple. A minimum wage law does not require the payment of the minimum wage specified. It merely says if the employer *does* hire the person he must pay that wage. If in the opinion of the employer an individual is not worth that much he is simply not employed. Considering the wide range of ability, dependability, physical strength, education, and other factors, there will inevitably be some "marginal" workers who could profitably be hired at 75 cents an hour but who would not be worth $1.00. Also we should note that there are marginal jobs as well as marginal workers. A householder will recognize a number of little jobs around his house or yard that he would be glad to have done at one wage, but which he will leave undone if the required wage is higher. A minimum wage of $1.00 merely adds to the list of unemployed any man who, because of low qualifications or low value of the job, is only worth 75 cents. From the point of view of the man and of society, it seems it is better to be employed at 75 cents than unemployed at $1.00.

Similar difficulties arise if government tries to raise the price of products. Less will be sold unless, of course, the government enters the market to buy unwanted goods.

Considering these and other difficulties, it seems to be a good rule to view the unfortunates as poor people, not poor farmers or poor workers. If we view them as occupational groups we will, for example, try to help a poor sharecropper by raising the price of cotton. Two bad results follow: First, less cotton will be sold and, second, the effect of the higher price falls on other unknown persons, many of whom are themselves poor. There seems no humanitarian purpose served by forcing a northern factory worker to pay more for his children's clothing so that a southern cotton grower can better buy shoes for *his* children. This way of trying to alleviate the conditions of the poor is self-defeating. But if we view these people simply as poor people without regard to their occupational group, the simple and generally the best answer is to provide them with money from the public treasury if it cannot be provided by voluntary contributions. It will, of course, be a "hand out," but on the whole it is probably better to recognize it as such than to conceal the fact by measures that distort the market system by wage or price fixing.

The direct solution here suggested will, for many reasons, not be popular. One of these is that much of the political pressures for the other solution comes from people who are not poor at all. When you raise the price of cotton to help cotton sharecroppers it may well be that more than half of any added amount paid for cotton will go to growers who are quite able to operate at the old price and make a good profit. In such cases the marginal producers may become only a front for the whole industry.

Needless to say, we are not trying to offer specifics for a relief program. Our purpose is merely to say that a philosophy of classic liberalism does not imply a callous attitude toward those who may fall so far behind in a competitive system that they require help. It would hold that the help should do as little damage to the functioning of the market system as possible and that a high degree of statecraft is required to give away money wisely.

Many efforts are being made by groups within our society to enhance security of tenure. Such schemes run into the objection from the general social point of view that precisely to the degree that some individuals obtain security in these ways, others are deprived of it. The schemes are always, in one way or another and to a greater or less degree, arrangements for the protection of those who are "in" as against those who would like to "get in."

The kind of security which avoids that conflict must be based on high and increasing productivity and high mobility. These two are consistent with the philosophy of freedom. Whether people will be willing and able to meet the requirements of each is the major question about security.

We cannot here go into detail. Suffice it to say for purposes of this essay that exponents of the free enterprise philosophy cannot afford to disregard this desire of people. Concessions must be wisely made within the general guiding principle of individualism, competition, and a free market, without doing too much damage to the principle. For, after all, security, as the other good things, is best gained in a free society.

Another feature of a liberal program is an extension of education. The point was emphasized before that there must be equality of opportunity for individuals to make the best use of the abilities with which they may be endowed. Until very recent years, and then only in certain favored countries, the kind and amount of education available to young people was determined by their station in society, by the economic resources of their parents, or by the special favors of the church or politically powerful individuals. By the existence of such limitations upon the opportunities for education, certain families and classes in the community could perpetuate their favored positions in the government and the professions. Of the various positive steps which can be taken to bring us closer to the ideals of liberalism, extension of educational opportunities would probably stand first.

The ideal should be that no individual should be precluded by economic or arbitrary limits from attaining such a degree of education as he can profitably use. There will surely be difficult problems to meet. For example, to what extent should public support of education be provided through federal, state, or local units of government? Here again the liberal ideal, generally, is best served when community action is kept as close to the people as possible. Also, there is the question, especially as to higher education, of how far we should expect young people to work for it. To say that they should be completely supported at community expense would, first, involve an extremely heavy burden upon the community and, second, it would mean the sacrificing of some of the educational values which many of us now recognize as inherent in the effort to provide for our own education. These and other practical and difficult questions must be faced; but the ideal remains that education at any level should be available to any person who is able to profit by it and who really desires it, and the latter proviso implies a willingness to make efforts and sacrifices to get it. This ideal should have the active support of true liberals.

Other lines of reform, such as improved public health, support of basic research, some forms of applied research, and others will occur to anyone of humanitarian impulses and will suggest that a program of classic liberalism is not to be identified with callousness or a merely negative laissez-faire policy.

One of the most important general requirements to be borne in mind is that any positive program of reform should remain as far as possible within the framework of general law. The rule of law as distinguished from arbitrary actions of even well-intentioned rulers and administrative agencies is one of the most important foundation stones of a free society and one of the greatest contributions to human freedom that has been made by the Anglo-Saxon and American people. Reforms in the various special areas will not represent net gains if they seriously impair this basic principle of our civilization.

As a practical matter, the contrast between a liberal program and an authoritarian or collectivist program is likely to be a matter of degree but not therefore unimportant. There has been much foolish talk, both by advocates of traditional liberalism and by those who lean to authoritarian solutions, in which the members of both camps have tried to define the other's position in such a way as to make it untenable to any reasonable person.

Let us try once more to define the issue in such a way as to avoid forcing the answer. Traditional liberalism as a practical policy implies that, in the solution of economic and social problems, the maximum of reliance will be placed upon the energies and initiative of individuals following the course of action which to them seems best; only to the necessary minimum does it rely upon the force of the state or the concerted action of interested groups within the society. Traditional liberalism relies to the greatest practical extent upon the spontaneous and natural forces of a free market and a free society; and only when these forces are clearly inadequate, does it resort to compulsion. A liberal policy is not a straitjacket, nor does it preclude the use of authoritarian methods when they are necessary, as at times they surely will be. But the liberal statesmen will place the burden of proof upon those who would resort to such methods; whereas statesmen of the opposite school of thought, when faced by any problem, think first of action to be taken by the state ("there ought to be a law") or labor unions, or farm blocs or similar centers of private power, and, only when those favored devices are shown to be too clumsy and impractical, will they fall back upon the solution of letting people work out their own salvation.

The authoritarian is partial to the use of direct action, i.e., to force (for good ends, of course). The classic liberal favors indirect action, i.e., persuasion and education and the slower process of raising intellectual and moral standards. He believes that mankind can raise itself to a level where individuals can seek their own ends and, at the same time, to an increasing but never a perfect degree, to so conduct themselves as not to infringe upon their neighbors' right to do the same.

He recognizes, therefore, that the great hope is for the improvement of people but also that restraints and regulations are necessary. As we said before in the liberal philosophy man is neither an angel nor is he a beast. His capacities for improvement and self government, i.e., government of himself, are great, and it is the highest role of a good society to give free rein and encouragement to them by the greatest possible extension of individual freedom. The opposite philosophy would go farther to protect him from his own follies and to substitute the judgment of rulers for the decisions of citizens. Despite practical difficulties in drawing the line, these two philosophies are opposed, and the opposition is not temporary. The clash of ideals has, in one way or another, recurred throughout the history of civilization and will not be finally settled in this generation or the next.

The Future

A doctrine of liberalism and the kind of society that it envisages are not for all people. As Lord Acton in his *History of Freedom* wisely said: "Liberty is the delicate fruit of a mature civilization." The Romantic philosophers who conceived that primitive man was free were no doubt wrong. The history of freedom is not one of a fall from some earlier happy state. Nor is it a history of continuous advance. It is rather the history of early partial conceptions of the free society among the ancient Hebrews, Greeks, and Romans, followed by almost total eclipse at some stages of the Roman Empire and in the Dark Ages, then a new flowering in the Renaissance, and another great advance in the eighteenth and nineteenth centuries. Freedom requires a high degree of political genius and care. It requires also a reasonable degree of peace and security from attack, for individual rights and freedom do not flourish in wartime. When the enemy is at the gates, individual aspirations must be subordinated to the common defense.

As the fear of the enemy bolsters human discipline and authority at the expense of freedom, so also does dire want. The growth of freedom and of liberal ideas has come among people who were well above the subsistence level. With most people the desire for freedom follows, in the scale of priorities, the means of subsistence. Patrick Henry's "Give me liberty or give me death" was, if it is to be taken seriously, the mark of a rare soul. A distinguished Englishman a few years ago, when asked what would be the choice of his people if they became convinced that the only way to avoid widespread unemployment was to yield up a substantial part of their civil and economic liberties, replied that in his opinion they would, before such an unhappy choice, yield their liberties. Insistence upon liberty is found among men who have banished abject fear. On the other hand, and not inconsistently, widespread freedom and individualism are in modern society the best basis of productivity and economic well-being.

We in America were fortunate in our national beginnings in an unusual combination of factors: colonists coming from the middle classes, bringing with them the ideals of freedom, and moving into an environment which enabled them to avoid the grinding poverty that debases but which at the same time offered a challenge worthy of strong men. Here were the bases for a free and prosperous society, and the growth of freedom and the advance of economic well-being supported one another.

In the history of freedom throughout the world the gains that have been made in some ages past were reversed for long centuries at a time; and this suggests that there is no assurance that this latest flowering of freedom will not, too, come to an end. The necessary conditions for its continuance and growth are most favorable in this country. We have the economic basis for it in the world's highest productivity and standard of living, and we have the necessary long tradition of free institutions.

Paradoxically these (affluence and the fact that our free institutions have become traditional) pose a problem. Affluence could lead to a desire to relax from the strenuous discipline of a free market. The long tradition of free institutions could lead to a dangerous relaxation of vigilance to preserve the area of freedom of individuals against a growing power of government. If we should slip back into a new dominance of individuals by the state or other power groups it would illustrate Arnold Toynbee's epigram that those civilizations that die, as most of them ultimately do, are not murdered; they commit suicide.

St. Norbert College Library
DePere, WI